PRAI

when I grow up i want
TO BE A CHAIR

"Ryan proves what's possible when we allow our vulnerability to take us beyond simply just living and into a vibrant and fulfilling life. This book is so real and raw that it'll inspire you to transform whatever your version of a chair is—and fly."

—Amy B. Scher,
bestselling author of *This Is How I Save My Life*

"Ryan Rae Harbuck made the brave decision to live at age 16, and 25 years later made the courageous decision to share her story. She doesn't have all the answers, and she is still figuring out life like the rest of us, but her journey is one we can all learn from, and open our view to struggles different than our own."

—Stephanie Kostopoulos,
author of *Discovering My Scars*

"When Ryan Rae Harbuck survived a harrowing accident at age 16, her mobility may have been limited, but her ability to reprioritize her life and flourish had not. Any one of us can learn from and appreciate this raw, often humorous, and compelling read. Now if only someone had thought to turn each of her chairs into thrones."

—Susan Triemert,
author of *Guess What's Different*

"*when I grow up i want* TO BE A CHAIR is both a heartfelt coming of age memoir as well as a work steeped in the wisdom and insight from someone who has been through the trenches and grown in the most beautiful and poetic ways.

Ryan Harbuck is a brave and masterful storyteller who expertly weaves together a combination of anecdotes and lessons through beautifully crafted words and emotions.

Ryan both thinks and feels deeply and allows her audience to take the journey with her, giving readers permission to reach into the depths of their own experiences and fears, encouraging personal growth from the deepest level of the soul.

After reading *when I grow up i want* TO BE A CHAIR, you will feel both tested and triumphant, while at the same time ready to reveal your own victorious and personal best."

–Tricia Downing,
author and 2016 Paralympian

when i grow up i want

TO BE A CHAIR

a memoir

RYAN RAE HARBUCK

OLD GOLDIE PRESS

To the three that changed the story for me. To Andrew,
Van, & Orren. I could never put together the words
that say what is in my heart, so I won't even try.

Just know, for you three—I am certain.

And—To Mom. To Dad. To Kelsey. I wrote about the
things that I needed to get out, the ones that held pain.
I know there were many moments in between where
the sun was bright, but that didn't beg to be written.
You may not understand it. You may not even like it,
but I want you to know that my love was with each
of you as I wrote it all. We will ALL be better for it.

PART
ONE

the escape

THERE WAS A SUBTLE KNOCK ON MY DOOR. It was supposed to be a routine Saturday morning, so that random tapping set off alarms in my ever-anxious and growing teenage cerebrum. But this was no typical Saturday nor setting.

"Want to go to the mall?" asked Adam, both breathy and nonchalant, through the newly ajar door. Adam was almost twenty, and that fact alone made him an attractive target for my barely ready-for-the-world sixteen-year-old self. How he clearly didn't care about anyone or anything else was also a significant draw. Not to mention the fact that he was constantly pushing boundaries further and further than he was supposed to. Especially in a place like this.

"What? Now? I don't think we're allowed to go anywhere." The words glided off of my tongue through the stark-white room that matched my stark-white existence. My mind had already decided that I was going to go.

"It's Saturday. You know nothing ever happens here on Saturdays," Adam said. "No one will even know that we are gone. We'll be back before your parents come, for sure."

Adam was right. Nothing ever happened on Saturdays. Even though there was an urgency to wake us up at six a.m. and get us showered, dressed, and "appropriate" for the day. Nothing else was going to happen.

During the week, they inundated us with appointments and learn-to-be-a-wheelchair-person classes (or perhaps that's just what I called them?) and doctors alike that kept time moving in its obvious forward fashion. However, the weekends were quite different. There were no doctors, no appointments, and nothing to distract me from the fact that I was living in a hospital.

Although well-thought-out in nature, my apartment-like hospital room was nothing more than that—a patient room with a mini-fridge and a pullout couch that was never comfortable enough for anyone to sleep on. A fancy lampshade that reminded me of some sort of Oz character, bold yet begging for any visitor not to see the truth behind the curtain. *What is that common saying? Something about a curtain or cloak over your eyes?* I imagine that it is meant as a reference to hide the truth and somehow soften the reality of the person behind those eyes. That saying is what I think of when I look at the lampshade.

I had made this room my home for about a week or so, but I could say with complete confidence that it was an enormous upgrade from my previous hospital digs. They had promoted me to what the staff referred to as the "East Side" because my body was healing enough to reveal some sort of light at the end of a long and underground tunnel that any claustrophobic person would absolutely refuse to drive through.

The "West Side" was the side of the hospital that you lived in when you first got there. You were hooked up to machines like a puppet that had completely lost its way. Over there, you shared a room with another patient that you shamefully hoped was worse off than you and had little family to bother you. Okay, you don't *really* wish anyone was worse off, but it's so hard not to compare your injuries and malfunctions with those so closely confined with you. There was a standard blue-colored worn, cotton curtain that attempted to divide your life from that of the person laying two feet away from you. It rarely worked at all.

Lucky for me, my lungs had healed, and I was gaining more strength, so I had found my way to the more sophisticated and progressive portion of the hospital. Sophisticated because there were actually things, like the lampshade, to make it feel like home. *Home, really?* They were still waking me up at six a.m. on a Saturday morning to help me get ready for my day of—*what?*

But now was my chance. Adam had asked me to get out of there, and I was going to accept his request, just not too enthusiastically. I didn't want him to think that I was a dork or anything. But before I had the chance to even overthink it, we were out the door.

My room was next to the elevator, across the floor from the nurse's station. Hearing the nurses gabbing in the distance, I knew we were safe to board. As the elevator door drew its ever-delayed close, I thought of all of those things one shouldn't be thinking when trying to be daring. *What were we going to do when we got outside? How were we going to get to the mall? Should*

I tell Adam that I've never been able to push up that hill next to the hospital in class yet? Were people at the mall going to stare at us?

People at the mall *were* going to stare at us.

Having only been promoted to the East Side a week ago, I still toted a rather conspicuous back brace made of thick, almost-fluorescent white plastic. In many attempts to hide the back brace, I had camouflaged my brace with stickers sent from friends and family who knew my desire to be more fashionable with my hardware. I hoped everyone thought that I wanted the stickers to make the brace friendlier and more eye-catching. But in reality, I wanted the exact opposite. I wanted the iconic Mickey, and Goofy, and Garfield & Friends to distract onlookers from what stood behind—a girl with a broken back and a body that no longer responded to her conscious will.

This same back brace, years later, would find its way to many apartments and mortgaged homes of mine, seeking solace amongst piles in garages and storage spaces. Looking back, I will never quite understand why I would hang on to it for all those years.

However, it did do its job. It held my spine in place when I sat. They instructed me to wear the brace at all times when I wasn't in bed. The thick plastic was less than forgiving and left blanching marks in front of my armpits and sweat stains. The brace was a precise mold of my torso, constructed for me a few months prior, a time when I was barely breathing and lacking life. Sometimes referred to as a tortoiseshell, the brace was created in two parts—the front half and the back half, which could be completely secured by three hinges of thick, white Velcro.

4

As the months wore on and I spent less and less time getting to be a typical teenager, the Velcro needed to be tightened more and more. My tortoiseshell became bigger and bigger, and equally less useful. Yet that tortoiseshell remained a great hiding place for my broken body. Every tortoise can relate, I'm sure.

But I am not really a tortoise. Not only was this back brace a complete eyesore for venues like the mall, it was also hard to navigate in. I had learned in class just the last week that in order to really maneuver a wheelchair in intended solid and forward motion, one would have to simultaneously grasp each wheel from as far behind as your arms could reach. Then you would have to lean forward to allow your arms to continue around the circumference of your wheel. The goal was to take your hands around as much of the wheel as you could in order to keep you from expending too much energy, taking little pushes, and of course, looking like a flailing idiot.

This was definitely a different life. Being sixteen, I was extremely keen as to what would or would not make me look like an idiot.

When you are a kid, it's fairly simple. You watch what everyone else is doing, and you think you only have two choices. Either you 1) do it because it's cool or 2) don't do it because it's not cool. Or at least that's what everyone else made it look like.

It would take some fumbles and years later for me to realize that there are far more than two choices, and that being cool isn't all it's cracked up to be. Little did I know, I was learning so much about how self-confidence and a true sense of self is really the key to being "cool" right then and there. My insecurities and vulnerabilities were electric. But deep down, I was learning how to be the real kind of cool for myself.

But right then, at that moment, sitting there in that quintessential borrowed blueish wheelchair that my physical therapist says fits me very well, I wonder and question its "cool factor." Come on. I was sixteen, after all, living an existence that I neither wanted nor chose. And these things mattered more than my PT knew.

From where I sat, I couldn't be sure about much. Look around you, for the most part, and your friends will help you decide what is cool or not—chances are, without even saying a word. But, right then, I had very little to compare to, seeing as all of my friends didn't have even an ounce of understanding for this. From where I sat, it was pretty lonely.

Looking over at Adam in the elevator, it was obvious that he was cool. He exuded cool from his freckly pores. The fact that he was a pasty redhead didn't even deter his coolness—which means that he is actually extremely cool. He was about to be discharged from the hospital, and because of that had already purchased and was currently sitting in his own wheelchair. It was cool. He and his physical therapist had chosen a fairly high-tech, sleek model chair that allowed Adam to be nearly as free as he had been before his own accident. And it was white. White and shiny and bold, if you ask me. Being an avid skateboarder and snowboarder in his other, non-wheeling life, his new chair was almost like a fun ride to him. Within a matter of weeks, Adam had learned to jump curbs, and hop on one wheel, and turn wheelies like he was involved in an interpretive dance competition for transportation vehicles. He was extremely coordinated, but he was also gaining a lot of function back. I was extremely uncoordinated and extremely jealous.

We weren't the only two teenagers in the hospital at that time. In fact, many staff members whispered often about the fact that the hospital was nearly being overrun by teens. There was Heather, the cheerleader that fell from the top of the pyramid. Ashley, my old immature roommate who, with a similar accident story to mine, seemed to co-mingle much better with my thirteen-year-old sister. And then there was Greg. Greg dove the wrong way off of a cliff in Maui but refused to talk about it to anyone.

One thing for certain, I kept tabs on all of their progress, and it felt as though I was losing a race that I never signed up for. Each of these supposed companions of mine were making progress, exceeding my own. Heather was walking, Ashley and Greg were kicking their legs, and as for Adam, he had stood up in the pool. *What about me? When was it going to be my turn?*

The elevator made one final, definitive ding to let us know we were where we were supposed to be, or more precisely, exactly where we *weren't* supposed to be. We had made it to the first-floor exit with no staff in sight to stop us. This escape could have had more of a dramatic flair for Adam, I suspect. I imagine he fantasized about outrunning Judy, the overweight and under-exercised head nurse, as we pushed toward the doors of our freedom. However, that wasn't the case. In fact, the detection of the automatic motion sensors courteously held the door for us as we took our last final push to the outside world.

We were free.

The sun was shining in a brilliant reminder that I was still alive. It was now the middle of spring, and for the first time in my life, I took a *real* moment. I took my own moment to breathe in the infant blossoms. The fresh dew that had a scent all its own in combination with the soil and grasses of the strategically planned courtyard in front of the hospital. For the first time, I realized how much time I had lost being inside the hospital. The last time I could remember being outside unsupervised, it was winter, and its icy chill was something that in the past I had hid from. Now I just wanted to be reintroduced, like an old lover trying to make sure that I was making the right decision to move on. The sun warmed my face and forearms in a manner that nearly brought tears to my eyes. I had never felt this way before. It was like being alive for the first time. Everything was moving slowly and with great purpose. And all for me to experience.

I was trying to not to get caught up in the moment of acknowledging that no sixteen-year-old should feel this way about anything. *Or should they?* I shook it off and followed Adam down the cemented path. Thank goodness, I had been down this sidewalk before in class and knew where to watch for bumps, and humps, and cracks. Those deformities in my walkway could make me regret my retreat with Adam if I fell.

Adam was already whizzing down the hill in his shiny white-painted, stealth bomber of a wheelchair in full wheelie position. Flying by rocks and cracks and mislaid gravel, he had no apparent fear.

I always was afraid, even before my accident, and didn't need a new wheelchair or rocky collision course to create more for me. I swallowed hard and shouted at myself to stop being such a sissy. Traveling down that sidewalk was going to be the least of my concerns. Adam had already wheelied ahead to the traffic light and pressed the crosswalk button to wait for his turn. As I approached, he found uncertainty in my eyes.

"You okay?" Of course, I was okay, but I couldn't help shake what happened *that night*. This was my first taste of freedom since that night. I was okay, but I wanted that sunken feeling to fall off of me.

"I'm fine. I'm okay. I'm g--," The word *good* couldn't quite make it out. I was never very proficient in lying. I shook my arms, thinking that would help. Adam just raised an eyebrow and pressed the button again, eager more than ever to cross the street.

Too often, I tried hard to remember that seemingly innocuous, peeping moonlit night that guided my body as I flew. Crashing and flying through that tempered glass car window, I knew I could survive much less. However, the dramatic slow-motion version of that fateful night, I flew so much that all that was left was shattered glass, horns alarming, and blood pooling. But no memory whatsoever. Although barely breathing, I was told that I was lucky to even be alive. So, yes, of course, I was okay just crossing the stupid street.

On the other side, we met a city bus with smiles. We had no money, and our only shot at making it to the mall was to appear as pathetic as the bus driver wanted us to be. This was a far simpler task for me than it was for Adam. Look at me—a sticker-laden back brace, mounds of metal all around, and the remaining scabs from events that only one could imagine. I donned a fresh pinkish-purplish scar attempting to be hidden by my golden locks that lay softly around my right temple. Moving my hair from my eyes, the defeat of days past shone through them. My blue eyes had dimmed since that night, and I feared I wasn't the only one who noticed. I nervously smiled to the driver, my unintentional gapped-teeth, and child-like smile. Somehow,

Adam knew I would be our ticket on that bus. And so I was, scars and metal and all.

The driver of the bus was now an accessory to the crime as he loaded us on the mechanical lift that made me even more self-conscious than the Mickey Mouse stickers waving at all the spectators in the aisles. Our chairs were firmly strapped into the floor of the bus with worn and intentional, yet lazily, planned seat belts that were stowed beneath the passenger seats. We were on our way.

The mall was about a twenty-minute ride, although it felt like much more. Adam and I traveled in silence, which led me to believe that he was, too, a little anxious for our adventure. As the bus whirled by familiar buildings with familiar smells and sounds, everything felt strangely different. It was as if I was seeing my hometown for the first time, or as through entirely different eyes. *Is this how an archeologist would feel as coming upon a new discovery in long-abandoned sand?* I could only guess.

We passed playgrounds where children played and laughed. How I ached to be in their shoes. We passed by banks, businesses, gas stations, and markets. I wished to be a customer or employee working dead-end jobs, or really any of them out in the "real world." As I passed by this world that was neither contained in a hospital nor confined by a wheelchair, I felt desperate to be anyone but me. Living life in a hospital, you rarely get to feel or witness anything remotely close to real life. And now I realize why they keep it that way.

Screeching sounds of neglected-to-be-oiled wheels brought my thoughts back to the present. Adam and I were unshackled from the bus floorboards and sent on our way.

As the bus pulled away, I felt it pulling at my gut. We were at the mall, far away from any familiarity and far away from any help. Shaking off my effervescent fears, I followed Adam through the parking lot that appeared to have doubled in size over the few months since I had last walked through it.

The mall was a mess of people, strollers, and shopping bags swinging directly toward my head. I had forgotten that there were so many ramps. I had never paid much attention to those things.

The mall was shaped in a long line of shops that cascaded from one giant hill, which caused the construction of an appropriately graded ramp nearly every thirty feet or so, which made one way fantastic and the other way nearly impossible. Perhaps had I more strength or less of a decorated, plastic tortoiseshell, I would be able to manage the ramps on my own. But it was immediately clear that I wasn't going to be able to.

This was to be one of the most valuable lessons that I ever learned. Right then, I knew I was going to have to do two very scary things: Figure out another way *and* ask for help. The ingrown lesson of figuring out another way was not the one that grated on my soul. Hearing the echoing notion in my brain over and over again, "you need to ask for help" was one of my ruinous concepts. My world felt upside down ever since my accident, but this felt just downright unfair. I didn't want help. I didn't want to need help. And I certainly didn't want to ask for it. Unfortunately for me, this wasn't something that I could just grow out of easily.

I already felt I had lost so much in my accident. I didn't want to lose my last remaining drop of independence as well. Asking someone for help would certainly tarnish all the adolescent milestone medals of honor that I had proudly adorned over the past few years. I learned to successfully drive a car by myself, hold a job at the local car wash, and even open my own checking account in my name. I was on the road to becoming an independent adult, and I wasn't about to make that U-turn.

But, for the past three achingly long months, I did move backward. I did swing into that U-turn. I did lose an actual sense of my self. I was forced to become completely reliant on others to bathe, dress, and care for me in a way known only to my former infant self. Being sixteen, you take all your effort to show the world that you can do it—and do it without anyone's help. And now, I had to ask a nurse to help me sit on a toilet.

I swallowed both pride and fear and asked Adam to help me. My thoughts were confusing. *How could I not manage a ramp on my own and expect someone else in the same position to help me?* I asked for his help anyway. It was most likely a *very* pivotal moment for both of us.

My grandmother used to tell me that putting the word "very" in front of a word actually seemed to lessen the intended impact. However, in this case, it was, in fact, *very* pivotal. Adam was in the trenches of learning a lesson about masculinity and regaining independence, while I was in the middle of learning a more subtle, yet powerful, message of true human independence.

For the first time since the accident, I was feeling what life was really going to be like from this borrowed wheelchair of mine. Life would never be the same, and I was going to experience many more instances of needing help up hills and over obstacles. I was going to have to be okay with that. I was going to have to learn to smile and appreciate the fact that the mall had even constructed these ramps in passive courtesy for this new identity of mine. I was also going to have to learn to have the guts to wander off to confront those ramps in the first place.

Likewise, I was going to have to learn to be patient and courteous to others, even when I didn't want the help or desire the company. I was going to have to learn that my life was going to be different than I would have ever imagined it to be before.

As Adam and I paraded through the mall and caught the attention of every eyeball in the place, I let all the insecurities of my newly broken body fall in the distance behind me. Those insecurities, although following uncomfortably on my tail, were not taking me over. And, because of that, I was free to laugh, and play, and feel like myself—that self that I had abandoned on the side of the highway with the rest of my uninjured teenage body and brain.

The day consisted of rolling up and down the long stretches of mall walkway and winding through and between clothing racks. It was also about becoming increasingly aware of the fact that everyone was, too, becoming increasingly aware of the both of us and our wheels. The stares and gawking gestures were muted because we were together. I felt as if I was less of an oddity with him because Adam was cool. Sitting next to him, attempting to emulate his smooth moves, made me cool too.

The sun earlier had helped shape and compel my emotions during my escape, and its descent marked the end of our adventure. Just as we had done before, we found a bus, pathetically played and hoped it to pay our way for the ride. We strapped our wheelchairs into the bus floor just like old pros, and headed back through the crowds of buildings and lives being lived outside of a hospital.

Moving in silence after a long day of successful discovery and rediscovery, Adam followed behind me, locking the front end of his chair into the back end of mine, just as he had done the entire day. We moved in unison as one force. No one else around us could come close to understanding the importance of such a simple outing. And no one could understand how important, ultimately, this moment would be for our own recoveries. At the time, it was just a simple outing to the mall with a friend. But as years wore on, it proved to be a crucial stepping-stone for me.

A stepping-stone for someone who no longer
knew how to take true steps.

The motion sensors acknowledged the two of us with open arms like a cheery grandmother with fresh baked goods and a red checkered apron. The immediate transformation of mind was almost frightful. After spending an entire afternoon remembering what it felt like to be a teenager and a human being, it took one simple push in a doorway to take that all away. The elevator sang and dinged its song of obligation. That song would later haunt my subconscious and remind me about these earliest moments, seemingly just when I required them most.

Those dings would forever remind me of the beginning struggles of this new life I had. Those dings could both frighten and comfort me moving forward, beyond that beginning. The final ding sang and the doors parted to a world that I had hoped all day to never quite make it back to.

A swarm of queen-bee and mother-hen nurses swarmed the two escapees to give them the reprimanding of a lifetime. There was at least a dozen of them squawking, gnarling, and grunting words of punishment and anger in a virtual slow-motion dramatization. It was like one of those programs that you see on television that takes place in the wild savannah where brilliant elephants, giant rhinos, and dancing zebras are all taking claim and stake over the watering hole in one ferocious, fell-swoop. I could do nothing but refer to Adam, for I was not the trouble-maker type and hadn't the slightest understanding of how to handle a situation like this. I just kept squinting, keeping my eyes low and wavering in hopes of missing direct contact with any of the beasts because that would be the end of everything.

I opened one eye at a time and gazed into the eyes of those caregiver nurses that were gnarling and gnashing. I felt something new for the first time in my sixteen years. I didn't feel as bad as I think I should have.

Wait a minute, I didn't really do anything wrong.

Okay, yes, I had left the hospital unchaperoned, without prior consent. I had made an array of women who had come to love and care for me as their own worry like crazy. But I also did something much, much more powerful too.

Taking that first step, or push, or whatever, out of those motion-sensing, dinging doors gave me a fragment of myself back. The hospital, although responsible for my ultimate recovery and progress, was also responsible for taking away my sense of self. I needed desperately to find that before any doctor could discharge me, call it good enough, and send me on my way to outpatient therapy.

As the dust settled and the safari animals quieted, both by the annoyance of defeat and their exhausting rants, hugs were exchanged. They sent me to bed without dinner, albeit with tired smiles. That day represented everything that might lay ahead of me. I was content knowing that I was still alive, and the world was waiting for me to come outside again.

jeremy

THE SILKEN BABY BLUE DRESS was resting on the bed, both avoiding the chance of being wrinkled as well as obtaining a stain of something–dare we say–hospital-related. I sat, squinting, trying desperately to make everything look different. But I didn't know what I really wanted it all to look like anyway.

I was in the oversized cave of a bathroom built with wheelchairs in mind, alongside two of my best childhood friends, Allie and Rebecca. Allie was complaining of her itchy pantyhose, and Rebecca was doing what Rebecca did best. She always tried extremely hard to be the one that appeared to care less while actually caring most, so she had positioned herself naturally between the mirror image of me and my own real self. I was attempting to both hold myself upright in my wheelchair while combing my preset curls, sweating profusely and trying to play it off that neither was that big of a deal. My balance had come a long way in the last few months, but I still had a horrendous time with the simplest tasks, which felt more defeating than gratified.

Rebecca played both the role of tomboy and princess to a tee. She exuded an air about her that was both alluring and repulsive. And, even though she was one of my best friends, I was dreadfully afraid of her. While staring into her own image in the mirror and perfecting those sweepy bangs that she mimicked straight from the latest Seventeen Magazine, she questioned why I was being so quiet. Truthfully, I was surprised she even noticed.

Allie had moved on from the bathroom, still complaining about her pantyhose, and had plopped herself on the couch to wait for the rest of the group to come. She was one of the sole reasons that Rebecca could get away with her attitude. Allie was mousey and awkward in every way, and was nearly always waiting for Rebecca's approval, of which she never got.

Why did I put up with this? And why didn't I see it before? Everything looked different to me these days. It was like I was a different person gazing, undetected out of the same eyes that matched that baby blue dress. The same dress was now sitting bunched and wrinkled on my newly frail-seeming body.

Living in the "East Side" of the hospital made this occasion a bit more bearable. The makeshift apartment-wannabe was the perfect teenage haven, especially when there was no other option. I had gotten my back brace off for good, just days ago. It was not a moment too soon for me to enjoy my first department store full-length gown at my very first-ever prom.

After my fiasco at the mall, it was a wonder that the nursing staff even agreed to let me go at all. But I suppose they saw it as an opportunity for me to try on "real" life for size. Little did I know that this sort of *size* had changed drastically since the last time I spent time with my friends. In return for being allowed to leave the hospital for several hours, I not only had to agree to take various pills and precautions with me, but also enlist my date in several extensive courses on how to take a sixteen-year-old wheelchair girl out for a night. *How embarrassing.* Thank goodness I was just going with Rob. He was sort of like a brother to me these days.

It's ironic, though, to think that Rob is like a brother. Rob was Rebecca's twin brother, yet you might not suspect it outwardly. He was very different than Rebecca in both looks and personality, and I was drawn to both. He was lean and gangly, and spent most of his time trying to be both funny and liked by all, especially when it came to Rebecca's friends. Although they got along well enough to sit within the same social circle, Rebecca's friends became Rob's friends by default. This, I suppose, led to the inevitable—one of Rebecca's friends would fall for him eventually, if he hung around long enough. That friend ended up being me.

Rob became my very first real boyfriend back when we first started high school. He had been the first boy to show any sort of romantic interest in me, and creating a secret relationship that required us to meet at set times in my moonlit backyard to avoid anyone finding out was reason enough for me to pursue him back.

Attempting to hide our midnight relationship from the world, Rob would tag along with Rebecca to movies that I would be invited to and "coincidentally" sit next to me in the darkened theater. These occasions would be nearly the only chance we had at anything resembling teenage dating. We would sit, stiff as stone, looking directly at the movie from opening trailers all the way through closing credits, with hands hidden and held underneath the sticky, plastic armrest.

As one can probably assume, once that relationship was found out and the surreptitiousness of it no longer existed, neither did the attraction on his part. It was easiest for me to play the same, as not to seem like a weirdo stalker or something. So, I returned to being Rob's sister's friend solely.

However, as emotions typically churn and yearn in settings of shock and upset, Rob started showing up at my hospital bedside nearly every day since I landed there. Once I became more mobile and relatively free of the complications that take names like pneumonia and Staphylococcus, it became more of a possibility that I may actually attend my junior year prom after all.

Rob asked, as if it was destiny, and I accepted it as so. From there, we spent several days and classes together learning how to actually make this night work. Everything was planned out, and the nurses gave their hugs and assurance to ease some of my anxiety about the evening.

I had nothing to worry about, right? I was going to have to learn how to live outside the hospital walls at some point, so I might as well get a taste of it in a silken baby blue dress, I suppose?

What I hadn't taken the time to obsess on, unlike all the other three million scenarios of disaster I had laid out in my imagination, was that I was about to attend a school dance again. For the first time since then. That's "THEN" with a drawn-out E–the one in where you are already supposed to know what I am referring to and react accordingly.

The last school dance I had twirled at was just about four months before, and subsequently, was the same night that I had twirled through the air and landed in this hospital.

Blinking hard, I looked back at my reflection in the mirror where incessant hair combing was turning into subtle reminiscing. That last school dance had been the last dance for me, but it was truly the last everything for Jeremy.

Oh. Oh, no. Now I couldn't stop blinking. Those blinks were keeping my eyes from swimming away. *Sweet Jeremy*. He was the young love of my life, and I couldn't wait to show him off in his father's borrowed, sophisticatedly striped navy-blue tie.

Jeremy was my then boyfriend and a perfect mix of feather and brick. He was a shy and reserved teenager until his comfort kicked in and told him to smile. His smile was an unforgettable stretch of innocence and sensitivity brilliantly spread across his well-chiseled jawline. He was a football player by stature but a neonatal heart surgeon by sensitivity. He was tall and broad, yet incredibly unassuming, and often played the part of wallflower to the rest of his peers. I enjoyed him instantly and spent as much time as I could learning about this boy who towered over most but rarely spoke a word.

We had been friends for months before I even had the slightest notion of his attraction toward me. My circle of girl friends had stumbled upon his circle of boy friends on a stale summer night where there was little to do other than start some trouble.

Our trouble was that we saw a car full of boys driving in the same direction that we were. Although we had no destination, we played it off like we certainly did. Without complete foresight nor hesitation, I showed that carload of boys a bare side of my back side. I didn't really think they would follow us, but they did. And lucky for us, it was the early 90s and the worst thing we could think of about that all is that we wouldn't like any of them. We actually ended up liking them all. A lot.

The two carloads became instant friends, and we were nearly inseparable the rest of the summer. With all the fun we sought out, it took that entire season for me to notice Jeremy noticing me. But, once he finally got the nerve to ask me to be his girl-friend, we couldn't get enough of each other.

It had been six months to the day, and we chose to celebrate that teenage success by going to the high school's winter dance. I had coerced two of my girlfriends from the swim team to ask a couple of Jeremy's friends to the dance, so that he would be surrounded, strategically, by a crowd of comfort. For this wall-flower, I would do just about anything. That would be the last time he would ever be near that sort of comfort in his life.

The accident occurred as most tragedies do—without warn-ing, without reason, and without forgiveness.

Some debate took place among state troopers as to the actual date of the accident, seeing as it was the stroke of midnight on my side of the world. Midnight is, indeed, a strange time. It is a time that is not quite tomorrow, and it isn't quite yesterday either. Midnight is the hour where you should be tucked neatly between your sheets and snoring lullabies of dreams to come, if you ask me. However, this was not the case that night.

While most of the world slept, we now fought for our lives. Each of the six of us that had piled in that car, together, yet totally alone. There is little sense to be made about how each of us fared, only that some were rewarded with more luck than others.

It was one second that changed everything. Everything for me, and everything for my five friends. We were sharing this

22

destiny, and everything for each one of our families. Living in that one second–that one midnight second–everything changed for our world.

The night had taken Jeremy's last breath as he felt his final impact on the cargo door of the sports utility vehicle borrowed from my friend's father. I was told that there was little struggle and no hope, for he was killed instantly.

He would no longer ever have the chance to get his driver's license, make another touchdown, graduate from high school or college, meet his future wife, rock his children to sleep, or tell his family he loved them one last time.

I think we are always trying to make sense of things, sense of the world, but what that night taught me with the force of a million fiery suns is that you simply can't. I have never been able to come up with any reason, rational or otherwise, as to why Jeremy was taken from this world. I have spent so many days thinking of the life that was never intended for him, feeling both horrified and thankful all in my own same ironic, life-giving breath.

I was told of his death extremely subtly, almost as a comma to an otherwise uncorrected run-on sentence. I remember the moment clearly, which is interesting to say, because everything else I recall during those first few days was equivalent to a reflection in a mayonnaise jar. As those words hit my broken body, I took those words in as little puffs of air, slowly, but comfortably as though I had heard them before. Nobody needed to tell me this news. My in-and-out state of consciousness honed in and picked up the news nearly when it happened.

But now, I was actually being *told* the news.

Someone decided it was my time to hear it.

Somehow those words were old to me now.

The feeling, though, was still ever-fresh within me. *How do I react? How do I make a face like it's the first time I've heard of Jeremy's death? What is that tube in my throat?*

But first, I had to even make it. I had to at least make it to the hospital, and I was told that the notion of little hope had swept over that accident, seen like the thickest blanket of fog one could think of.

While struggling for my existence on the pavement of the now-bloodied highway, I was completely conscious, or so I had been told. My self-coddling brain had washed any inkling of this event firmly away with bleach and discarded it in the garbage of some lost memory. I remember nothing of my accident directly and very little for about a week afterwards. I suppose, this was probably one of my greatest saving graces. However, learning of my consciousness in the midst of the blood, and screaming, and downpour of tears was shuddering.

I actually learned of Jeremy's death exactly as it happened in real time. No one needed to tell me, dramatically, standing over my own broken body hooked up to tubes and machines. But, they did so, and I was intended to react to it.

I didn't know how to understand everything. In less than a moment's time, my entire life had disintegrated into ashes of dreams and memories drifting weightlessly away from me in the foggy midnight moonlight. It couldn't be so. This didn't happen.

With the help of a cocktail of both shock and morphine, I was able to make sense of it all in a disaster-relief sort of way. During the days in the hospital, I was kept busy with my own healing and learning about this new life. I found things to distract me in ways that were almost comical.

Just over a week after bursting through the ER swinging doors, I somehow found it absolutely necessary to create handmade Valentine's Day cards. The holiday was only a day away, and my resurrected infant mind thought nothing more important than to make cards for all the doctors and nurses that visited my noisy, monitor-beeping room every day.

My mom would bring stamps and gobs of colored papers in pastel hues that she had lying around the daycare center where she worked. She thought stamps would be a good idea because I was truly too weak and broken for much else. *Just one more heart right here—I can do it.* My eyelids would repeatedly fall shut from pure exhaustion.

I have always been quite motivated by using crafts as a small attempt at connecting with people. I am not always the best with words and confrontations, but I can do wonders with a pair of scissors and some broken oil pastel pieces.

When the hustle of the day gave way to darkness and a lull in visitors, both those desired and the ones necessary, I was left alone to heal and to dream. At night, I was free to roam about my consciousness and find a more settling existence. With the help of some very strong sedatives, each night I would dream in colors, and sounds, and smells of life. This made it increasingly difficult to discern my current reality with the one that I longed for.

In my dreams, Jeremy would appear, usually through a phone call, assuring me of his return any day now. He would give me glimpses of the vacation that he was having in Arkansas with the most clear and realistic tone. Jeremy was laid to rest in Arkansas. My brain wasn't too far off.

Brains are powerful instruments when learning to cope. They can take over and steer you in any direction necessary for your own survival. I suppose I should have stamped a Valentine's Day card for my own brain, looking back.

Jeremy would promise me that he was coming home, and we would go out to the movies or some other teenage rendezvous that sounded so good. I wanted nothing more than to see him smile and hear that stretching sound your mouth sometimes did when you are really smiling.

We would spend hours, it would seem, each night catching up on our days, laughing, and planning our reunion.

Each morning I would awake with my familiar smile, but to the hospital tech and his consistent whistle and expected breakfast tray.

I have never been so disappointed in my life.

There was no need for me to share my conversation from the previous night with anyone because all that mattered was Jeremy and me. Besides, I was so worried that someone would tell me that I was wrong, or delirious, or stupid. Or worse. I was worried that someone would have to tell me that Jeremy was gone all over again.

The night before the prom with Rob, I had my usual reverie with Jeremy, but this time it was about my real-life anxieties. I expressed my desire for him to be there and my, what truly felt like, rational understanding that Arkansas was too far away for him to get back in time. I assured him that everything would be alright and that I would share everything with him afterward. That night, in my dreams, Jeremy and I spoke for the last time.

I was preparing to let him go, and I didn't even know it. He had kept me alive through my darkest hours in the ICU. Through relearning to breathe off of a ventilator, as well as through tears of the excruciating pain of daily skin sloughing my road rash to cleanse away any harmful infection, I kept him with me. He, his image in my mind when I closed my eyes, kept everything tempered and okay. He even kept the chasing demons that screamed, "Why me?" virtually voiceless.

Thank goodness for Jeremy.

But now it was time for him to go.

As our dates arrived through the elevator, just outside my hospital room door, it was clear that it was time to leave. That final elevator "ding" brought me back from my mind and its illusions. Allie had now become increasingly antsier, and Rebecca had gone back to the bathroom mirror a dozen more times, smacking her lips together and kissing her image as the finale. The limo was waiting for us all downstairs, as were my parents and the entire East Side nursing staff.

We all said our farewells, and the limo driver circled around ambulances and hospital staff out for their evening smoke breaks.

As we rode further and further away from the hospital, I became more and more aware of not only the new life I was about to be granted, but also of the one that I was still holding onto. And I was desperate not to let it go.

I sat in the limo, chilled from the fresh air that my body hadn't been used to. Looking back toward the hospital, as we drove away, the song on the radio did little for me when capturing that memory. I'm sure there are very few 90s songs that would have fit that moment at all. Or any songs, for that matter.

Although we had said our goodbyes in my dreams that last night, Jeremy prevailed and showed up at the dance. Oh, how I cringed at the very thought. *It's not real. It's just in your head. He's not here. He's not ... anywhere.*

He showed up just long enough for us to exchange glances and smiles, yet no one else was quick enough to notice. My cringe returned as he now left my sight. *It's not real. It's just in your head. He's not here. He's not ... anywhere.* The chant almost became somewhat of a mantra as I scanned through the crowds.

As the night wore on and the music strung together couples in sporadic tempos of dance, my glances of Jeremy became even more slight and sporadic as well. And as the glances eventually became fewer to none, my gut protested in desperation. I hid in the bathroom, in the giant handicap stall, away from everyone—both real and imagined—for so much of the night. I wasn't ready to lose him forever, and that pit inside of me said it so loudly. But I knew it was imminent. It was now. Something within me, although having never experienced anything like this before, recognized its purpose. It was time to say goodbye. Again.

That night was the last night that I ever saw or heard from sweet Jeremy. I never saw nor heard that wide smile anymore. I never felt the gentleness of that giant ever again.

In my short teenage lifetime, Jeremy had managed to die in front of me twice.

tough skin

"YOU HAVE REEEEEAAALLY UGLY LEGS. Did you know that?" The soft, yet sharpened young voice said from below me. Taking a big breath in, both for time to gather myself as well as a corrected answer to this nosy five-year-old, I looked down at her.

"Yes. Yes, I know. Now are you working on blowing bubbles like I asked?" I supposed I had better just get used to it. I didn't blame this little wet, goggle-faced inquirer. She didn't mean to twist and rip my heart, but she did it all the same. I needed to find some tougher skin if I were to survive this new life.

I swallowed so hard it hurt.

Ugly! The girl said that my legs were ugly … .

Science has proven to us that beauty can be found in items of pleasing symmetry. When visualizing such symmetry, it is easy to think of the contrasting monarch butterfly and its paint-by-number wings. Butterflies are beautiful, so those scientists must be right.

Why are these people so set on making sense of *everything*? Can't things just *be* anymore? There are emotions that don't have proper words to explain them, I'm sure. And, in that same respect, there are things too powerful and important to be explained through equations or formulas. Science can't adequately describe the things in my heart. I know that.

Beauty is something that is unique to each person and often has a direct correlation to their experiences and past acquaintances. Expressions of beauty should be left alone to be uncovered as they will, but who would find beauty in *me* now?

When I look down at my disproportionally atrophied legs, I see no sort of symmetry, not even a glimpse. I see the leftover gashes and slashes, covered rather conspicuously by the scars that healed there in the same manner mold grows if you leave something in the fridge too long. A belly button-shaped scar tells me about the time my tibia bone broke through my skin in one treacherous blow. I saw grafts of immature skin that should never belong there in the first place and a silhouette of a calf that looks rather like a shark attack, complete with missing chunk waiting to be digested in that imaginary shark's belly.

I suppose you *could* call that ugly.

Scars are formed by cells that specifically repair at all cost. Those cells lack elasticity. Those cells cannot smile the way our normal skin cells do. Scars are tougher and darker, and do work as the best Band-Aid we will ever know. However, those are the same scars that I have tried to hide not only from the world but also from my own eyes. Those scars are not only the motive behind frightened children and pointed fingers but also the most obvious and demanding reminder of that night. Not that I wanted to totally forget about it, but I might chase forever just trying to not be reminded like this.

It happened without great care and with little mind to consequence. It happened in one beat of a heart—that notorious "lub-dub" of heart walls clapping in unison and the joy to be alive. It also happened purely without intention—a mistake, an accident.

As though in a courting display of both dominance and excellence, that oversized car flew. Little was understood about the precise manner or motive of flight, but the six-passenger SUV caught flight as birds do. In soaring, it seemed capable of breaking barriers of both time and mass, wreaking havoc in its direct paths and its aura around. Each of the six passengers began their own stories of anguish and struggle, yet each was now forever bonded by a single moment of accidental flight.

My personal flight did not end with that of the vehicle. I was to take a second, more monumental and vulnerable flight of my very own. Apparently, the universe saw much more for me and kept me rocketing through that midnight shadow far beyond the wreck site, and far beyond what my body could handle.

On the outside, painful, skinned traces and reminders as I leapt against the cold pavement. Inside, contrasted with crushing bones against one another until the momentum let me go. By the time I finished flying, my body had already started dying.

Blood poured relentlessly from a single slit in my forearm as it signaled rhythmically and directly from the pressure of my heart. The blood was pooling and growing around me. This same blood that kept me dancing and smiling just minutes earlier with Jeremy—was now killing me through its defined departure.

Neurons fired out of control, like fireworks over the ocean, causing one giant system-overload and one final, compulsory groan from my nearly lifeless breath. All the energy I could muster created that one muted groan with the potential to be lost in that very midnight shadow that laid me down not so gently just moments before. But it was, indeed, that slight groan that saved my life.

With little confidence in their capabilities to revive a life that was seemingly ending, first responders felt the hopes of reaching the hospital in time were ticking down. Something inside of me was not willing to let go, and it held on to everything it could, as life was literally rushing out of me.

I'm not sure if I held on to past memories and moments or if I held on to the faith that there was more to come. Whatever the case, I was able to grab hold of something so tightly that the risk of losing it all shattered with the image of something much stronger than death. I wasn't going to die, not because it wasn't my time, but because I did not *think* it was my time. Lying there, in that sixteen-year-old body covered in blood, I made a brave decision to live.

With fingers crossed, I made it to the hospital on a newly soiled stretcher and an extensive list of broken bones, from clavicle to fibula. The blood that had been lost needed to be replaced and quick. The now shiny, weeping skin exposed on my back needed immediate attention. Being sloughed off from the road, it oozed to try to keep me alive and free from additional harm.

A doctor barked orders down the hallway, echoing demands to "prevent potential bacterial invaders," "prepare an OR room STAT," as well as "someone stop the bleeding." My awareness of it all was pulsating, in and out.

In and out.

The tube that had been placed strategically downward deep into my pharynx and deeper yet in my trachea required a more permanent solution if it were to continue to help my body battle for its own existence. There was little escape from injury on any single part of my body. It is a wonder that the doctors had enough supplies, speed, and hands to tend to everything that my sobbing body ailed from. It was truly like my body was weeping uncontrollably, fighting hard to find someone to comfort it. 'Please save me,' it whispered.

Beyond the newly exposed skin layers and deeper than the broken vessels that poured the crimson flow of both life and death, there was a delicate pull of my spine and crushing disconnection that was going to soon be the thing that changed everything.

From the manner in which I flew, it seemed virtually inevitable that my spine was going to suffer somehow. Even though that injury was, by far, the most life-changing, it was, ironically, my legs that needed tending to first. If the doctors didn't brace the crackled and displaced mess that once resembled those very things that allowed me to stand tall, I would have no chance at life whatsoever. They were bleeding from inside out and the outside in. Truly, my legs would be no use to me again. But the fact was, I was going to die without them.

Five hours later, my legs represented something like an old historic building that would have fallen apart from its own accord. That building, though, was important to someone, it seemed, so anatomical architects threw money in the way of shiny new scaffolding and mortar to make the most immediate attempt at keeping that structure standing. *Hooray! We saved the old schoolhouse!*

My legs were now part of an erector set of bandages and metal holds. It was days before I would actually recognize the severity of the condition of my legs, or the severity of what had happened to the rest of me.

It is true ... time heals all wounds in the most literal sense, for that is clear. As for the metaphorical implication, I can't quite speak to it. The time that it took to heal my body was fleeting, yet the time that it took to heal my soul was immeasurable.

As that harder, less elastic cousin of our epidermis, scar tissue, takes charge in the fiercest sense, it will undoubtedly and hastily salvage what was waged in war. Designed to ensure gashes and gnashes, stabs and jabs eventually go away, my body grew scars everywhere. Yet, no matter how unsightly and over-stated, they kept me alive.

Even though I am terribly grateful for their work, it would be nice if I could forget them, and all about that night, even just every once in a while.

Being sixteen is hard when you have little to differentiate you from the rest of those nervous sixteen-year-olds. But that was no longer the case. Not only did I have daily reminders of that night and all that was lost, but so did everyone else. I was the visual aid and constant reminder of that night for everyone. It wasn't long before my friend that drove the SUV that night couldn't bear to see me. It wasn't long before other friends shied away as well, simply because they didn't know what to say. Even my own family.

Having the insecurities that go along with being sixteen, I wanted to rarely step outside of the hospital doors on most days. I wanted to cover up in a blanket, pulling its comfort downward on top of my body, close my eyes, and think of running through a grassy field. To this day, that image and fantasy of running across a pasture or sandy beach is always something that serves me. I say it serves me, but there are equal emotions of love and disdain mixed in that image.

I spent most of my time alone trying to convince myself that nobody cared about my wheelchair and that it wasn't thought of as a burden or an oddity. I was still just me. *But who am I anyway?* Some days this worked, yet others, I was still just a teenager struggling to fit in a world that just shockingly became far less accessible to me.

I couldn't hide my wheelchair—that was evident. But that's not to say that there wasn't a valiant effort to do so. When placing the order for my own very-first wheelchair, my physical therapist urged me to pick a bold color that would stand out.

"Do they have a see-through one?" I was only slightly joking. I settled on forest green—one, to appease my PT's effort for me to normalize my chair, but also because that shade of green is like the one kid that got left out of the class photo because no one remembered him.

Once I managed to get over the fact that I couldn't have a transparent wheelchair, I started focusing on the things I could hide from the world. I could hide my legs, and I could, for the most part, hide from them as well.

I made some fairly conscious shopping purchases of longer-than-necessary pants and knee-high socks, which were neither cool nor in-style but far better than the alternative. I spent so much of my time concealing my legs that it quickly became habitual self-detriment. And that habit quickly grew like a wildfire inside of my pubescent, introverted mind. Along with all the hiding, my self-esteem hid too.

Hiding became a way for me to ignore confronting what had happened to me. I kept an arms-length away from most people too. If I didn't believe in myself, how could I expect anyone else to? If I didn't find myself unique and important for it all, I wasn't about to make others see it that way either.

And, just when I thought those feelings couldn't get worse, there was definitely one place I couldn't hide my legs from the world. Pained me beyond comprehension. Ironically, it was also the only place that I ever wanted to go. It was the only place that I could feel I could get away.

It was the swimming pool.

In the pool, I didn't rely on my wheelchair, and I could roam about virtually unnoticed under the lifeguards' towering view. It was a haven and a bridge that connected my old life with my new one. It was the only connection that I made between those two, clearly separate lives of mine. Having little memory of the night of my accident, it was fairly easy for me to compartmentalize my being. I had a life that is now gone, and in its place, I had a new one.

But if I wanted to actually get to that point in the pool, floating beneath the world above, I actually had to get in first. I would unintentionally hold my breath for as long as it took me to lower myself into the pool. I suppose I hoped that if I didn't breathe, no one would see me. I actually didn't exist. I would force every muscle in my upper body as the most riff-raff of teams to lower me into the pool, shaking and weary from doing the job of all extremities. I tried so hard to show little struggle and as little emotional strain as possible. *Don't make eye contact. Please don't look at me, and don't you dare offer to help. Don't make eye contact.*

It was one of those brief, yet never-ending, moments of breathlessness into the pool when I was stopped by that wide-eyed child with the unbelievable reputation of something more like sorority bully than an inquisitive five-year-old.

"You do have really ugly legs. *Very* ugly. I think they are scary."

I thought there wasn't anything that could have kept me from the pool, until that moment.

I didn't return to the pool to swim for weeks.

Years later, and numerous variations of the same remark, led me to a series of years where I pledged not to shave my legs. I thought it was much more as a protest of my nonconformity and inconvenience. But in reality, one day, it became grossly obvious to me that it was simply just one more way for me to hide.

Still today, I am so aware of the asymmetry and the gagging distaste I have for the appearance of my legs. Even though those feelings of shame and repulsiveness haunt me still, it is perhaps with much less frequency.

You still will not see me flaunting my legs around town or sporting the latest daisy-duke shorts, but I have grown to appreciate my legs for what they are and, even more precisely, what they will never be.

Yet, those scars did one thing. Those scars gave me tougher skin.

tuna can, trash can, i can

REBECCA WAS ALWAYS THE INSTIGATOR, and Allie, the clumsy one, got everyone caught. It was a priceless duo. There was a time in my life that I longed to be closer to both of them, but looking back on those days, I am utterly thankful that I didn't actually change to the point that I fit in fully with the dynamic of those two.

Some relationships are truly toxic. Believe me, I've had my fair share. Especially when it came to the time just following my accident. I would have taken attention from a rattlesnake if it thought that I was just an ordinary girl. I so longed to be normal and ordinary, but more importantly, seen that way.

For the remaining years of my life, I think "normal" is something that I will always strive for. I am not sure if I will ever come to terms with the fact that my life is and has been far left of ordinary. I try to avoid using the word "extraordinary," although it's probably an appropriate synonym in this context. I would much rather be like the rest of the faceless world around me. But for my newly injured teenage self, I'd befriend literally any character who found it possible to see anything beyond a wheelchair and battered body.

The summer after my accident, that's when I first realized that I longed to be normal. All that I wanted was to get my driver's license again with my new hand controls to power it. I wanted to break my curfew, just like the rest of teenage America. I was also hoping that my friends wanted the same, not focusing on the potential challenges that laid ahead just by being my friend.

While I was still in the hospital, my friends took turns during visiting hours interacting with my newly startling silhouette and wheels underneath. They would visit me with distractions of soda pop and magazines, with the juiciest gossip from high school hallways, and even once a goldfish in a clear plastic bag.

Unfortunately, it was the goldfish that sent me over the edge. With me bursting into hours of previously dammed-up tears, I peered into that puffy plastic bag filled with water and stared at the fish. He was trapped. I felt sorry for that fish, and I felt sorry for myself too.

Looking around at the bleak white walls of the hospital around me, I forced my eyes to look toward the ceiling, in hopes of cupping up some tears. I mostly just didn't want anyone to come into my room and catch me crying. Not only would it be extremely embarrassing and lame, but it might also cause someone to ask more about how I was feeling. I was definitely not up for that.

Easing my friends into my new life was pretty seamless on the surface, especially when we never spoke about the accident, the death, nor my paralysis. That dreaded "P" word. How long before I could say that word, paralyzed? Paralysis? Paraplegic? Ugh. All of those "P" words could just go away. I learned quickly to ignore my friends' unmentionable words too.

For years, I would recall myself naïve and young back then, but truth be told, I knew exactly what I was doing. Since just ignoring everything made everyone else feel better, I followed suit, knowing full well that I should retaliate. I blame myself for not being able to stand up for the new me. I couldn't stand up for myself with my friends. I couldn't stand up for myself with my family. To this day, I can't even recall a time in my whole life where either one of my parents have used the "P" words either. Perhaps that is where I got it from in the first place. I shudder to imagine.

Once I was discharged from the hospital and got home, it was quite clear that people were going to have to start talking or the emotional world may just explode. Although I was young, I was now forced into a world now that I didn't quite understand. I longed for someone to guide me toward what I was supposed to do and how I was supposed to feel. That someone didn't exist in my life. That someone didn't exist in my "basement apartment."

I became habitant to this shiny and new "basement apartment" which quickly became the envy of all of my friends, and particularly with my little sister, Abby. This wasn't shocking in the least, seeing as Abby was envious of everything that I had or was back then. And, I suppose on some level, even my accident.

This make-shift luxury apartment-like pad was constructed as a way for me to forgive my parents for not wanting to move out of our trilevel home in comforting suburbia. Stairs were no longer an option, and we had countless rows of them in my home.

The apartment became host to its own walk-in shower and vanity area, as well as a kitchenette with mini-fridge and microwave. All the while, it also held the remnants of the old basement that kept the washing machine and all of our Christmas decorations secured into specifically labeled boxes. There was a clean layer of concrete poured into a walkway that started at the garage and swooped all the way around the house and into the backyard, stopping just shy of sliding glass doors that soon became my only independent way of entry into my childhood home. What a fabulous metaphor for all the things I was feeling but couldn't put words to. That poor basement tried so hard to be something it simply was not.

I no longer sat at the kitchen table to do homework. I no longer ate dinners propped on wooden boards in front of the television in the family room. I no longer saw the Christmas decorations out of their boxes. I no longer saw the bedroom that I grew up in.

It was all upstairs.

Now all that I had was this dumb creamy-white basement apartment with brown-mud Formica countertops and an isolation that was unwarranted. All of my friends thought it was so cool to have this basement apartment. I wanted to think that too, but I just couldn't help but feel tucked away, like no one knew what to do with me. My chair, my new life, those things didn't fit in with the rest of my world. That trilevel house became my first taste of the real, inaccessible world. This inaccessible world was, unfortunately, not limited in solely physicality. Inaccessibility is a word that typically translates to location and navigation. However, I've woefully learned that it can also be used when speaking about more emotional, heart-driven matters too.

The summer held all the makings of pure brilliance: sunshine, no school, driving cars, best friends, and now basement apartments. Gaining some of my freedom back was made possible by my immaturity and longing to be just like everyone else. I learned how to maneuver my wheelchair without wheelie bars to keep me from falling, simply because I left them on top of Allie's car without thinking as we drove away one day. I learned that going up the escalator at the mall is much harder and quite literally painful when the staff from the hospital is not standing there to catch you.

Every single day I spent learning about what this new life was going to be like and what I was going to have to do to maintain it all. I learned about it just by living it. Everything seemed to hold such a greater significance, and I tried my best to smile for it. That new perspective that I built was hard for anyone else to understand.

More than anything, I felt completely alone. Not just because I was now living in isolation in my teenage jealousy pad, but also because it was extremely apparent that nobody else in my sit-com world understood any piece of what I was going through. I kept hearing that audience laughing track on repeat, with no actual joke being said.

I woke up every morning hoping to be awakened from a dream. I was scared and vulnerable to most things and most days.

I became a worrier and ridden with self-doubt and loathing. My smile kept the whole thing a secret from my friends and family. I had no one to tell, no one to understand, and no one to bring me out of it. I felt like only part of a whole person, and the part that was left was stinking and smelling up all the joy and wonders around me. Spending most days wishing for something else, I was absolutely consumed by my lifeless legs and equally lifeless self-confidence.

Every morning, I awoke nearly two full hours before the sun, just to make sure I had enough time to shower myself, dress myself, and encourage myself about the day. I often lingered in front of the full-length mirror nailed on the inside of my closet door, posing in awkward ways, attempting to make my chair small-ish and invisible. It never quite worked the way I wanted it to.

I noticed that my body had begun to change in that full-length mirror too. Each day my legs seemed a little smaller, frailer, and a lot more purple and hypoxic. My upper body began to change as well, as it had to play the role of both arms and legs. Blouses soon piled up in the closet floor, with buttons that no longer clasped, and even tiny rips in the tops of the shoulder seams. I thought I looked so strange, especially those legs. I tried to abandon them. "They aren't mine. They must belong to somebody else," I told the mirror me. She echoed that same thing right back. *She didn't want to claim them either.*

I blamed myself for not feeling like I could show my true distaste for my new persona with others. But on some level, I just silently wished that someone would understand. To understand would mean that they felt it too. No such luck. That was frankly not the case. My make-believe smile ordered both family and friends to go about their days as normal, passing by my emotions and secret cries for understanding on the way to movies and shopping malls. On the inside, I begged for someone to hear me.

That accident had left holes in every aspect of me. I was peering through a chain-linked fence, having much difficulty focusing on what lied on the other side due to the woven galvanized steel that created specific eyeholes for viewing. To peek to the other side, you could only look through *one* steel-framed hole at a time. Otherwise, it just got too difficult and unfocused. If the focus was on my wheelchair, I left out things like my absence of function or absence of mind. If the focus was my paralysis, I ended up paralyzing both my past and future at the same time. Attempting to gaze into the other side of my own existence, I realized that each of these holes are merely a piece of the *whole*, and without them, the fence wouldn't stand.

"My car smells funny," I remarked to Allie, not being able to help the strange way that her lip was curling upward toward her lie.

"I don't think so. Rebecca, you smell anything?" Allie called out to the back of my oversized, white beast of a sedan. Luckily, my grandfather had given it to me earlier that summer, as both a hand-me-down and a failed attempt at buying my newly broken, teenage happiness.

"Nope. Nothing. Come on, let's go. You are making us all late worrying about nothing." *Nothing.* Nothing, they said.

"I just feel like it has been getting worse. I noticed it a few days ago, and now it is definitely more … more … gross." I couldn't shake that smell. It was an obvious odor that my brain had recognized over and over again, but this time out of context,

I was completely baffled. Allie's notorious curling lip made me continue, "It's like rotting roast beef, or smelling socks with cheese stuck in the fabric ..."

We drove the rest of the way in silence, except for the apparent conversation that was taking place between my nose and the rest of my olfactory system. *What was their problem? Why did I feel like there was an invisible wall caught between them and me? Did that wall also keep that awful smell out, or do they really know something? Please don't let them know something. They are all I have.*

That night I returned home alone, still focused on that dreadful odor and the peculiar way that my friends wholeheartedly discredited the entire thing. My gut told me that they had something to do with it, but my heart told me that there would be no way that my friends could be so callous. Besides, what would I honestly do without them? I would spend my summer alone, more alone than I already felt. I couldn't handle the thought.

After unloading my wheelchair frame from the seat next to me, I attached both wheels, just as they had taught me to do at the hospital. Supposedly, that would get easier—they promised me it would. I reminded myself of this as newly exerted sweat trickled down both sides of my forehead. Before wiping away my noted efforts, I decided that I would take matters into my own hands. Just because I couldn't move my legs anymore, most certainly didn't mean that I didn't know how to smell.

Staying in the driver's seat, I pushed my upper body as far as I could extend toward the back seat. My torso felt a stretch that it hadn't in a long time. Briefly, I worried I was going to damage the metal rods that now lined my spine, but I forced that thought away as I sensed a stomachache coming on. Realizing that I had never more than glanced in the back seats of this car made me entirely distracted and disheartened. Making mental notes of a small oil stain in the carpeting and tire marks on the back of the passenger seat, I continued on with my search. I wasn't sure if I was going to be able to search how my brain intended, but I shut out those doubts and twisted even further around until my entire upper body had dove beyond the center console and into the seat cushion of the back-passenger bench.

Any physicist would tell you that such twisting and diving of one part of a structure will cause equal movement in the other part of the structure. My legs were following along with my hips, which were just following along with my back, which were following my newly developed shoulders. I had my lower body on a leash, and thankfully it obeyed. Soon, I had made a sort of bridged pretzel of my paralyzed half as the sweat continued to remind me of the new struggles of simple tasks that life had created for me.

Wiping the sweat from forehead to forearm, I shoved my only dry arm underneath my driver's seat. I struggled in the dimmed light of the garage, alone. My dad and mom, and even Abby, all seemed to go about their way inside, just beyond the garage walls that framed the family room. I wasn't about to honk the horn and let them know I needed help anyway. How fitting.

What was that? It felt both smooth and jagged, both circular and square. It was something I knew, yet I couldn't quite figure it out with my fingertips alone to navigate. Digging down deeper just one last time caught both my foot under the car pedal as well as my final attention.

I've got it!

Pushing against the backseat, I managed to push myself upward enough to fall back into my original driving position, but this time with ironically crossed legs. This proposed politeness over the cultivating profanities that were in part by the sweat, circumstance, and the surreptitious little can that had caused my nasal passages so much grief those last few days.

Tuna.

The deliberate manner in which the lid was raised reminded me mostly of the way that Allie's lip curled previously in the day. They *did* do it. But why?

It wasn't bad enough that I already felt like a terrible burden to all of my friends, but now they were going to sabotage my very existence in teenage coolness by playing a prank on me? My heart was pushed down inside of me, causing my breath to wane and my stomach to churn. It was the first time that I ever felt that emotion of betrayal. It was so foreign that I couldn't name it at the time. I did the only thing I could, and I shoved it in another known category of the moment: Sadness.

Truth be told, Rebecca and Allie had always been a little immature and a little more farsighted to things directly in front of them. But *after all that I had been through, all that I was going through ... how could they? How could they be so cruel?*

Instantaneous profanity turned to tears just as sadness turned into deep sorrow for all the events of the day and my new, unsettling existence. The odor of rotting fish immediately became a reminder of my own rotting life. I couldn't handle being poked fun at, not to mention lied to like that. They are going to tell me that they were just kidding. They are going to tell me that it is okay. But ... it was absolutely not okay to feel this way.

After sobs of loneliness and helplessness in the solitude of the timed-out darkness of the garage light, I forced myself to come up with a plan, a strategy. Now, this was neither a plan of retaliation nor a strategy to approach Rebecca and Allie about their doings.

This was a plan to rise above this smelly mishap and create a strategy to propel straight beyond its potential emotional potency as well as its actual stench. I finally sniffled away my insecurities enough to allow the tuna and its conniving culprits to dissipate somewhere beyond my nose and beyond my heart, far into that still summer night.

I let go. I actually let go. I let it hurt me just long enough to realize that the significance of this event ranged far beyond the actual reeking occurrence.

At that moment, in that air of warmed sea and motor oil, I began to trust myself for the very first time. I recognized the most permanent scar of my accident: my own childhood.

I no longer understood the meaning or desire for pranks. I was not willing to entertain such frivolity when there was so much more for my heart to engage with, or disengage for that matter. I did, however, feel the desire to resolve my sorrowed heart and simultaneously let go of those things that just didn't matter. I would carry this feeling with me, hold it under the night sky, and be better off because of it.

Not only did I feel a loss for my childhood that night, mourning the spirit of those notable twins—ignorance and bliss. But I also felt a loss for friendships that had been, consequently, outgrown. My accident had taught me too much about life as well as its converse to now be akin to most of my friends. That naivety was gone. It was gone for good.

In that instance of slamming my body from car seat to wheelchair seat, I felt a sudden change of foresight. The eyes that I was currently gazing out of, although neither damaged nor affected by my accident, were now able to see things that did not previously exist before. I was able to witness emotions and grab on to tones I once couldn't hear in one great embrace of the newness and acceptance of it all. I sighed. That, too, felt different and changed.

Although there was no actual difference to the world, how I had perceived it was unearthed and altered. And, even though the work that my eyes did to recognize the world remained intact, my brain now understood those sights in a much different, clearer sense. I had traded out my funhouse mirror for an actual, conventional, and respectable full-length version.

In the garage, I wheeled myself and chair over to the trashcan and gently dropped the tuna can effortlessly, allowing gravity to do the work. That can had reached its destiny, to join the equally foul likeness of toilet paper rolls and chicken bones. I wanted no part in expending that sort of energy. I just let go.

That tuna can was not the only thing that was thrown away in the trashcan that night.

reflections in an empty pool

THAT FIRST DAY BACK IN THE WATER was wretched. Being named a member of the lowest level swim group, after so many years of competing, was the least of my worries. I peered from chair to water and took a single breath in. That breath held both the strength of my desire and the fear of my uncertainty. I didn't know how to even get in.

Would I have to ask for someone to help me? But, who? I wished I was brave enough to just fling myself into that high school pool.

I scanned the pool deck nervously, and with a lot of help and a lot of pride-swallowing, I was lifted into the pool by my coaches and a few sympathetic teammates. Before my accident, there were very few people that I actually would let help me *with anything*. I was so determined to do everything the same as before and so scared at the same time not to be able to.

"Thank you." It almost came out of my mouth in pain. Not because I wasn't grateful for the help, but because somewhere in my being I knew that this was my new normal. I was going to need help from A LOT of people A LOT of the time.

Before I had the chance to let that lump in my throat grow, I held my breath in tightly once more and closed my eyes, entering the water.

The icy chill of this chlorinated dream felt like magic to my ribs and arms. My legs, although seemingly disinterested from their lack of self-propulsion, tricked the eye into seeming alive and dancing as I gazed down the lap lane. I was in the pool, and nothing in the entire universe was going to stop me from swimming—not the cold, nor my body could take me away from this bliss.

I tried to take the focus off of how grueling of an effort swimming had become, dragging over half of my body behind me. I also squinted to lose focus of the swimmers around me, with their terrible technique and affinity for splashing water as they sped by me. They gave minimal effort to whiz by me, and that made me so furious. *Don't watch them, that's not helping you.*

I tried, rather, to focus on the fact that I *was* swimming and I *was* normal. It didn't matter that my muscles could only sustain about twenty minutes of actual swimming, and my nervous system could only handle about five minutes of cold pool water before chilly convulsions piped in.

I was back in the pool, and swimming once again.

I was so determined to not let my newly challenged exterior get in my way. Focusing on my hands and how they pulled through each stroke, creating clinging bubbles, and familiar pressure to my palms. Focusing on my breath, slow and controlled, in the ultimate mediation for my soul.

I would not allow my self-deprecating, delicate mind to tear this moment away from myself. My legs were dragging and swaying behind me in a manner that was certainly hindering me. It was so hard to pull against such lag, but I didn't want to feel that. I didn't want to focus on that.

I was swimming, and it felt good.

I didn't need to rely on my wheelchair or anyone else while I was in the water. This was a first since my accident. I felt so light and so free. I felt like me again. I found out right away that my body could float. My new body, for the first time, didn't feel like it was holding me back. That feeling of weightlessness, the press and motion of the water surrounding me, and the low hum of the pool brought so much to my spirit. My body was being awakened as it moved around freely. My mind was being awakened too. That moment floating in the water became the only genuine connection I felt to my life before my accident.

I fought hard to find the normalcy that swimming provided. And, after I was able to let go of so many differences, and just focus on the actual freedom and serenity that I had always found with swimming, I was able to start moving. Moving forward, for the first time since my accident.

Letting go of all the things that swimming used to be versus all the things that swimming was with my new, paralyzed body wasn't so easy.

"Go, go, go!"

"Kick, kick! You can do it!" So many sounds filled my subconscious with memories and feelings I had never realized before.

My thoughts were quickly cut off ...

"I'm so glad you're here! You're actually here! Look, guys ... she's here." A familiar, but not friendly, voice came from behind me. Really, I didn't want to turn around to look. I just wanted to close my eyes and forget altogether about coming to the meet.

I offered up a soft wave, with enough politeness and sorrow to shut her up. I didn't want to see her or any of my teammates now. I was only here because I was a supposed-member of their team. But I was sitting in my wheelchair, parked in the stands next to the bleachers. The sounds lulled.

I had always loved the water, ever since my mother decided I would at three months old—simply dunking me under, letting go, and watching my infant survival skills bring me back to the surface. With the desire to fuel an innate sense for competition, and not wanting to chase down any more stray balls, I turned to swimming as both sport and identity.

Just before my accident and world came crashing in on me, I had made the varsity squad for the third consecutive season, and I had set my sights for the big State Meet. Had I known that my swimming career was going to be halted by this one ephemeral event, I may have done things differently.

Perhaps I wouldn't have had so many excuses, mostly driven by my lack of self-confidence. Perhaps I would have actually believed that I had the talent and allowed my ego the pride that others displayed and I was so desperately jealous of. Perhaps I would have actually let myself love swimming, rather than just endure it.

But now, I sat in my wheelchair next to the rest of the spectators and parents who actually could sit in the stands. This meet was considered an outing of sorts for me. Sure, I was formally a part of the team, but no one knew what to do with me—including me. So, I watched when all I wanted was to be a part of it.

I just wanted to be a kid again. Little did I know that would never happen again. An accident like that changes you, and it changes everything and everyone for you. Take those snobby swimmers that now pretended that we were friends. They were still kids. They didn't understand. *I just want to remind you, I never signed up for this.*

"You look so good!" One overly peppy teammate bounced over to me from where the rest of the team was sitting. However nice it may have sounded, it stung to my very core. It brought me directly back to the present with a sort of bad taste in my mouth. *I don't look good. I don't want you to think I look good. I don't want to be here. Look at me! I mean, really look at me.*

She had her swim cap on, and mirrored race goggles rested on her forehead, in the exact position to allow an exact reflection of myself in return. My reflection was so sad and confused. *How will you ever belong? How will you ever let yourself be good enough now?*

I smiled at my teammate, hoping that it was enough of a reply for her to shut her up. I smiled at my lame reflection in hopes of giving it some sort of power to move beyond this moment. *It'll be better someday, I hope.*

Luckily, my goggled teammate thought little of the interaction and bounced her way back to the rest of the team. I felt lonelier than ever. When I was sitting there with the uniform crowd of blue and red teammates, I felt lonely enough. And now I was actually sitting outside of the crowd that I was supposed to call my team, and I wanted to utterly disappear altogether.

I didn't belong in that sea of blue and red. I never did—even when I was smack dab in the middle of it. But it wasn't anyone's fault but my own. I guess I chose not to belong.

There was always something I felt about those "really good swimmers" that kept me from achieving more. *It wasn't any of them, it was you.* They completely intimidated me, both dying to be like them and dreading the very thought of it. And now these girls are the same ones waving for my attention. *My* attention.

Before the accident, I fought hard not to have to swim with them in practice, which helped me to have little interaction with them. With *them.* That mindset also catapulted me to a place of no confidence in myself and abilities. Often, my coach would move me right smack in the middle of all of them. Panicked, I would swim fast (but not too fast) and spend the rest of the time shutting tears out of my goggles.

I would fight my way back to a slower lane, a lane that felt comfortable and safe. A lane in which I could easily be the best without the worry. Before my accident, I was never up for the challenge. Before my accident, I was safe—yet completely scared.

I think I was actually scared of living.

Probably one of my biggest regrets, and probably one reason coaching similar swimmers became a passion of mine later on, was that very insecurity. When I had the chance, and able body to back it up, I hid and ran from my dreams. *I was such a wimp back then.* I would have been so annoyed with that swimmer if I were her coach. If I were her coach, I may have seen it in her though. I would have pushed to get it out of her so that she didn't have to live with that regret. That she, being me, did have that regret though.

Regret can be such a powerful fuel in choosing paths to take and roads to cross. As distasteful as it is, regret can play a useful role in finding one's best life in the end. That regret that I felt was helping me to see that I was the one to blame for that lack of confidence.

The roar of the crowd had somehow faded into a dissonant hum swirling over my head. I was lost in my mind, a very lonely and unforgiving mind. All of a sudden I had so much time to spend in my own brain. I don't remember that from before the accident, at least not with the same frequency.

Looking down toward my lap, my body was changed from the carbon-copy swimmers cheering in front of me, and I felt more lifeless and flaccid each day. I had spent dozens of weeks lying in a hospital bed, counting dents in the ceiling and peeling away scabs on my knuckles. Although important to my overall healing, those weeks completely deteriorated my muscles to where I could no longer lift my head off of the starched straight, bleached white pillow that sought to deny me the very sleep I needed.

By the time I was well enough to sit up, I could barely flex a muscle, let alone push a wheelchair anywhere but in a straight line on a smooth surface.

After months and months of physical therapy, I was now, indeed, gaining muscle back in my arms and shoulders from where they had hibernated while my body was just trying to stay alive. My arms were now working overtime and without pay.

My leg and trunk muscles no longer felt the electric connection with my brain, though they ached to be reunited. They would gladly begin working again if given a chance—even pro bono, no doubt. But that connection had been permanently lost. Those muscles in my legs, although still very much alive, withered to almost nothing because they didn't have the control panel of my brain to tell them to go.

As scars were building up on the outside of my body, the muscles lying beneath cried for attention. My body had become something almost unrecognizable to me, which was frightening and embarrassing. I sat, fiddling and fixing my team sweatshirt across my lap. Though this was more than skin deep.

I couldn't help but watch race after race, focusing on only which leg muscles flexed off the block of each racer. I narrowed in on everyone's kick and the powerful white water that flung itself as a direct result of the effort. For the first time, I paid close attention to how swimmers got out of the pool, stressing their backs as they pushed on the rusting metal gutter in one flawless-seeming motion. Everything in slow motion, and everything amplified a gazillion times.

Everyone's legs were so beautiful, with smooth and stainless skin and the beauty of a thousand marble statues. The way everyone could just move and jump, the way they sat on the ground so quickly and then got up again. It all looked so easy. I used to do that too.

I was so jealous of everyone. Not only at the swim meet, but everywhere. I hated being a spectator. No longer an active participant in any of it. *What am I even doing here?* I just kept my half-smile and wave going for everyone else's benefit and for my chance for it to tell them, "I'm okay."

I sat virtually in silence throughout the meet and kept trying not to pay too much attention. I didn't want to know who was swimming my favorite races, and I most certainly didn't want to know their times or the places they came in. "I could have beaten her, and her, and maybe even her, if I tried hard enough." *Oh, that regret. It found me again.* It entered my body and left me sinking deeper and deeper into my shiny new wheelchair propped next to the wet bleachers.

Catching my blanketed gaze was that reflection again. This time, it was lurking in the puddle on the ground, growing on the cemented pool deck in front of me. Race after race, and splash after splash, it had finally grown large enough to reveal me again.

The angle of the reflection exaggerated my wheelchair, almost like looking directly into a spoon. I gave myself a little wave, although it looked more like a brush off from the puddle-view. That sorrow came back—I couldn't even make my own reflection feel better. *I'm sorry.* I stared into that puddle just as it was a part of me. It was me. Hiding, virtually unnoticed in the stands at the swim meet.

As the meet ended, I did as I only knew and gave high-fives and hugs to the supposed teammates of mine who were exhausted, hungry, and complaining about both. Oh, how I longed to be them. Any of them. Even Beth with the zits and Lauren with the bad grades and consequences to match. Those things you can fix. Zit creams and after-school study sessions, see? Done. Problem solved. *But look at me.* What are you going to do with a paralyzed sixteen-year-old wannabe swimmer in a wheelchair?

The crowds shuffled out, and I waved goodbyes to cocked-head sympathizers. I suppose there is something innate about that subtle head positioning, being slightly tilted with saddened eyes. That head cock made my heart sink. It made it so because I felt the unrelenting pity from the unintentional participant. It radiated from their face, crushing down directly on my heart.

There I sat in the rarely quieted darkened pool area, surrounded by a low swirling sound of the water drowning into the gutters. The meet had ended, the crowds and swimmers had dispersed, and my mind was completely consumed by the "if *only*" ...

If only I had trusted myself more.

If only I had tried harder.

If only I didn't care so much about what everyone else thought.

If only I had let swimming feel this important to me before my accident.

My mind constantly reminded me of those things that I didn't have anymore. I had lost all my grip and was weakened by the thought of it. I tried so desperately to hold on to any piece of it, pinch it tightly in my palm—but it slipped away, to somewhere I no longer knew. I hadn't set out to live a life of regret nor live a life that I didn't want. I had to do something.

Just then, something flashed in the corner of my eye. It was that same reflection. She smiled at me without the pitiful head cock. That smile, it was *me*.

I could still swim—and although it may not be how I had it before—I wasn't going to settle on a life that I didn't want by being unresponsive.

No matter that the life I was now sitting in as a foreign-feeling spectator, it was there in that empty pool, staring back at me. There was a new sort of me, staring deeply at the reflection in that chlorinated pond—half familiar and half unknown. Staring straight back at myself, my new self, I realized very transparently that I still had a life to live, and that it was my job to determine both its value and worth from that point forward.

Those faded faces in the bleachers had left to their dinners and prime-time television programs. Those wet and hungry swimmers wrung out their hair and thought little of the ease of pulling on their team tracksuit before walking out the door. And as I sat in an empty swim meet, with empty surroundings, the water appeared to flow in unison with my mind.

Reflections from every part of my life beamed toward me. I was ready to recognize that my life was just that, mine. Although it wasn't exactly what I thought it would be, nor wanted it to be, it was still *mine*. Regret or not, it was now my job to make it something great, empowering, and worth everything. Every penny, every breath, and every second of every piece of it all.

That subtle and solitary moment changed everything.

For making that unintentional decision to move forward and to push through the water, using its resistant nature to move my body forward has become one of the most powerful lessons I could have ever dreamed. Breathe in and breathe out.

I was now ready to move forward in my new body, along with my new mindset of the world. I was ready to be something and someone that I hadn't ever imagined, yet didn't quite know had existed in me before either.

Having the will to accept those circumstances and moments that guide you, whether intentionally or otherwise, holds a secret that can propel you further than ever imagined. It can move you in the direction of a life that you wouldn't have ever dreamed possible. How do I know, you ask? My reflection once told me so.

to be a chair

YOU ASK ANY FOUR-YEAR-OLD what they want to be when they grow up, and the answers are relatively predictable: *doctor, teacher, firefighter, astronaut, veterinarian* ...

Having the desire to impact the world at such a young age is paramount. Setting goals of accomplishment– "Mommy, I'm going to the moon for lunch!" is a remarkable skill to fulfilling all of one's fairy-dusted, not-yet-tainted dreams.

At a young age, my parents were at their best, or so I'm told. One of my dearest friends, from the old neighborhood of swing-sets and barbecues, remembers my family as the photo-perfect family at the middle of the cul-de-sac. It would be akin to Betty Crocker and Norman Rockwell consummating their own down-home and home-cooked relationship, I could imagine.

Indeed, we were outwardly so. We were all blue-eyed, blonde-haired cookie cutters from a family sit-com mold. However, those are the days that I don't recall from memory nor nostalgia, unfortunately.

Something that I learned from my accident is that your mind has the power to block out things—memories and events too powerful for your consciousness to carry. *Is this why I don't recall more from my childhood? Was it tragic, or simply too mundane to cherish?*

From what I hear, my parents were taking on their sit-com roles and assuming the now unbelievable positions of both Mother and Father of the Year. My mom, especially, was primed and up on all the latest parenting jargon and methods of the minute. She swore to never give me any sugar, yet by the time my sister was born, one of her first words was, "McDonald's." And, try as they might have, they clearly created a different world for both of us kids. Our differences, even today, are stark. While I was always set to a totem pole standard of goodwill, good work, and good deeds; Abby somehow was compared to a garden gnome, that is, if we are creating valid outdoor statue metaphors. It was always that way. But I'll never be sure why.

A spectrum of contrast between the two sisters, in both expectations and directions. Abby grew up interested in clothing, parties, and how to get into trouble. I, on the other hand, grew up burrowing my head in my studies, swimming, and being that person who my parents just assumed me to be. I suppose I did offer my fair share of trouble to them, although most of it was unintentional. Likewise, I also honed in on my own, self-imposed expectations, as my parents never uttered words of forced encouragement nor woeful motivation.

However, the differences between Abby and me were apparent to everyone. I couldn't help but constantly wonder *how* we were so different, and how we would grow—together or apart—as we, in fact, grew.

Abby wore her immaturity well. She worked a room with it, and people paid attention. I suppose that is why she grew up how she did—or didn't.

As we both fell nearer to adolescence, it was a wonder if we would ever get along. Everyone sort of falls toward their teenage years because it was something you just do, like gravity, with little outward effort. It just happens.

Abby made it her own life's work to get me into trouble, while I attempted to maintain my head high and beyond any of it. Or at least that's how it felt. Those three years that separated us felt more like dark and cold choppy seas, taking days to show up at the shore as an actual tide. I could barely even see her from that ocean's distance.

I recall Abby chasing me around the house with lofty threats. I remember her displaying her own bite marks to my parents just to try to incriminate *me*. I never remember her trying to be anything other than plaguing to me, but perhaps that was my own lack of sight for such unassuming things.

Then there was my mother. My mom was terribly slender, almost painfully, as she sat eating her plain baked potato and dressing-less salad each night. Alone. I had never genuinely noticed that she did so alone at the table, after we all had finished our own comparatively lavish meals, that is until it was too late to change it.

She spent her days taking care of Abby and me, along with various other kids in the neighborhood. I always thought the other kids were great fun. It was like having my own Hasbro Real Baby Doll every single day. I always enjoyed helping my mom take care of the younger children at her stay-at-home daycare, and perhaps that was one of her best parenting moves of all. It taught me maturity and compassion at a young age, as well as tolerance and genuine selflessness.

I suppose I should have seen her uncertainty and anxiousness earlier than I did. I'm not sure which she could be more proud of, taking care of so many kids as her own business venture, or staying a size 0 through all of her adulthood. That, I suppose, should have been a sign to me earlier. With constant remarks of how "fat" she was growing up and her inability to eat so much as a sandwich with us, it was no wonder that her general unease couldn't be contained and oozed into more and more of her life. But I always knew that she loved me. She may not have always loved herself, but she always loved me.

I didn't always blame her.

My dad had a work truck and came home each night after the sun had already set. I have nostalgic and fond memories of awaiting his arrival, sitting perched upon the bay window benches, singing songs of Michael Jackson's greatest "Bad" and "Beat It" to pass the time. I still think of dancing on those cream velvet chairs when those songs come on. For as long as I can remember, my dad played the role of the stoic and passive stronghold of the family. As a kid, I can't even remember hearing his laugh.

I suppose that it wasn't always that way, and it certainly isn't that way today. But it took me a long time to see that my parents had feelings and emotions. And that they were both very, very unhappy during those gravitationally pulling years of mine and Abby's adolescence.

My dad spent most weekends on the golf course. Abby and I thought it was so extraordinary though, when he would take us to the park to work on our own batting swing. Baseball with red plastic bats was far more thrilling to us than golf. It should have been for Dad too.

His furrowed brow resembled his same, furrowed mustache—which he wore my whole life. That mustache was a staple in his life and in our family. It had its own place at the dinner table. *Who am I kidding? We never sat as a family at the dinner table.* My sister and I had our plates full on tiny TV trays in front of whatever program it was to be for that nightly routine. While my dad, tired from spending all of the daylight at work, sat in his leather easy chair. From afar, my mom would sit, one level up, in the kitchen eating her rabbit food, alone, separate from the rest of our separated family.

Back then I never fully understood the importance that basic conversation, actual talking with one another, could be. I never knew how much I really missed it, because I never had it.

It wouldn't be until my adulthood that I would be privy to seeing my dad in the same light that his golf friends did. As a kid, I would hear them remark at how "funny" my dad was—and I felt almost betrayed by such a notion. *How could it be? He couldn't possibly know what funny is or how to even be considered such ... could he?*

However young and naïve I was, I always understood my dad's love for Abby and me. When he preached to us about the entire purpose of our worldly lives simply being "to make ends meet," it made me both undeniably disgusted and overwhelmingly loved at the same time. My dad only knew one way, and never knew how to get out of that grimly hole doubling as a shallow grave he had dug for himself the day he decided to surrender to his "ends."

I didn't always blame him.

Yet, I truly believe that I am the absolute best of both of my parents.

They gave us the freedom and liberty to make our own decisions like any good parents would do. I recall never knowing my parents' political views nor any views at all. That fresh slate, unlike most parents, gave Abby and me the opportunity to grow and foster our own beliefs of the world. I was able to learn and develop my own thinking from a myriad of sources. From soft-spoken teachers to loud-mouth kids on the playground, I learned a lot. And informative television propaganda whilst propping up my TV tray to less-informative influencers like Rebecca and Allie, I also learned to develop my mind.

Truth is, I fear that this technique of my parents may have been more out of a lack of self-confidence, decisiveness, and overall presence than anything else. But, regardless, I was free, was able to think freely, and mold my own ideas of the world.

Playing the role of the older sister, I taught Abby everything I knew as soon as she was old enough. I taught her how to eat slugs with one quick "*slurp!*" I taught her how to hide between cornstalks, ensuring getting hives by morning and an utter freakout by Mom, who swore that we all had the chicken pox for the third time that week. I taught her how to share the swing in our backyard with me and me only. I enjoyed teaching her the things that I could as a way to share all the things that I had learned from others.

In part due to my mother's whimsy and my father's late nights at work, I had created my own thinking from as young as

I could remember. I will be forever thankful for that. I initiated make-believe like there was no other way to believe, and it wasn't long until people started asking me what I, too, wanted to be when I grew up.

My honest, doe-eyed reply?

I wanted to be a chair.

In those preschool years, I spent my mornings playing GI Joe with the neighbor boys, with whom I had completely assimilated. My afternoons were whisked away by sundried, painted pasta necklaces and radiant, invisible friends. I was definitely a child full of learning, and yearning, and wonder.

Enjoying my crayon-box scented days like record albums spinning around a primary-colored, plastic record player, I had it all. My soft, airy locks gave me just enough flighted stature to bounce the highest atop my pastel floral comforter. Conversely, at times, I would choose to hide under that bed and floral comforter with the company of all of my favorite Madame Alexander porcelain dolls—the untouchable ones, or so my mom and grandma thought.

Every day held more mystery and prose than one small child would ever realize. Yet, I took for granted the luxury of such imagination and free thought. Not to be muddled by insecurities, or those girls that whispered behind you in the hallway. Sometimes I wish I could go back to my preschool self and tell her that she had it pretty good.

Now, jump forward a dozen years and imagine the horror of your four-year-old fantasy being lived out in the most sordid of senses. In attempts at connecting back to those days and that innocence, I often have questioned my mother and her lucid sanity in allowing her little golden girl the ability to aspire to be something as mundane and inappropriate as a *chair*.

My mother would later explain to me that the tone of certainty and pride that I chose to disarm my dreams, she couldn't dare challenge them. And so it was.

For a solid year and a half, I wanted none other than to be a chair: an adult-type, sit-on-me-all-day-and-never-get-sore kind of a chair.

In the most rational sense that I can find, I can only determine choosing such a career due to my desire to hold one-year-old baby Abby and never getting that wish granted. Such premonitions don't really exist. Do *they*?

There must be a tiny flicker of rationale to ignite that explosion of foresight. Regardless, at that toddling point in my life, I was so proud of my aspirations and would do everything in my power to live up to my dream.

Little did I know the universe was listening to every single word of it.

There is something beyond powerful about the manner in which life unfolds and displays itself for each of us. There is something even more powerful about actually accepting it and learning from the winding and uncertain path that you journey forth.

Everyone has their own path, and maybe it dead-
ends at a shiny, metal chair. Maybe it doesn't.

The trail will be blazed by those things that you love and those things that carry your passions. This trail will contain light dustings of hope and deeper cracks of defeat. This trail will leave behind specks of our experiences from every day of growing up. This trail will always lead us home, if we so choose. And that "home" may be different for each one of us. Perhaps this path has no end, and frankly no beginning just after the moment you take that step ... and that step ... and that one there too. Perhaps this trail, this path, is nothing more than you.

And, as for this golden-haired girl, it would be ridiculous to think that the universe was granting me an eccentric childhood dream. But what if it was?

After all, it's not the chair that made me *me*, but it is the chair that made me *be*.

●

clenching can'ts

FOR SOME REASON, Wes always saw me as beautiful, probably in some of the same ways that I found his unrealistic teeth endearing or those silly overalls as unique. He was never afraid of the things that I couldn't do. In fact, he was always willing to challenge those things with a thick-toothed smile. And off we'd go.

Wes entered my life not a moment too soon, for I had already begun shutting the door on experiences that I felt unreachable and naïve of me to dream about. Just as there were only cracks of the sunshine created by opportunity, Wes came into my life to tell me, "*Why not?*"

Unbelievably seamlessly, I had graduated from high school. Looking back, I suppose there were probably more than an ample number of empathetic teachers who worked hard to make it so "seamless." With equal ease, I attended the local state college, without so much as a star-spangled standardized test to entice the admissions office. Was that empathy contagious or something?

Everything was good. Everything was normal. I loved school. I hated school. I went to school. I found other things to do instead. I met a lot of friends. I got rid of a few too. I had done such a good job at being the "normal" college kid that I tried so hard to be. But then I got sick.

It was my fourth year of college, again.

I had transferred to a college closer to my hometown after being hospitalized a few months because of an infection that my body couldn't quite attack all the way on its own. It was always one of the hardest parts to deal with since my accident. An alarmingly frail and aging body that wasn't at all suited for the newly twenty-year-old mind that demanded it.

Still, I packed up my "oh so normal" state college life and headed out for a new one. Bon voyage. Good luck to me.

Being my fourth year, my supposed last year of college, by the time I got out of the hospital, everyone had nearly vanished. My roommates and friends had all since graduated and were embarking on their own new journeys. They had scattered all around the globe to begin such remarkable things. As for me, I was being reminded by my own back-stabbing body that I was not ready for such greatness. I was bound by some insignificant credit requirements to finish what I had started. But I didn't want to stay in a life that had packed up and left. So, I left too.

I moved into a little apartment near, but not too near, my family and my childhood home. I settled into the nearby university to finish my studies, which were to take me an entire year just to make up for the lost time. Lost time in the hospital is a separate subject of its own. It was only a semester that I was away, hospital gown in tow. But it was going to take at least two semesters-worth to get me my degree at this new school. Being used to disappointments, I didn't linger much on the notion for too long before classes had begun and a new routine had set in.

I met Wes by happenstance. Not only had I seen him in a lecture class that I had earlier in the day, but he also became the student-teacher to my anatomy lab, and an instant confidence confidant in my latest world of uncertainty. We shared a convoluted relationship of both friend and mentor for quite some time, until neither of us could bear it anymore. Wes graduated after one semester of sharing the campus with him, which then enabled him to invite me bowling. Within only a couple weeks, bowling turned into dinner, and dinner turned into so much more.

Wes had grown up with his own problems and the suitcases full of buried emotion to match. I think that caused him to live a life for only him. He lived to challenge his body and mind, and from the moment I met him, I learned the same for me as well.

We would spend mornings in fields of wildflowers and even wilder bugs. In the afternoons, we constructed elaborate plans of how I was going to tube down the creek at this specific eddy and not drown before Wes could catch me downstream. We even spent many a summer evening wrestling with an unreasonable hammock, attempting to hear the elk bugling in the distance, just because I had once suggested it.

Wes was my refresher course in living, and as a result, my fondness for him grew quickly and brilliantly. He was capable of showing me that there was a world waiting for me that I never had the guts before to see existed. But also, and maybe more importantly so, he was willing to make all sorts of adaptations and accommodations just to ensure that I would be there by his side. I couldn't think of a better love story. *Who could write that kind of stuff for me?*

For all the love and confidence that Wes folded neatly in his daypack for me, it came as the coldest shock when he questioned my self-proclaimed sense of adventure.

"You can't go abroad. Why Venezuela? Uh, it's really hilly, and dirty, and ... you just wouldn't like it." Each word was a separate, newly sharpened dagger to my still very fragile heart. Wes became a toddler having been given a giant cookie with M&Ms baked in—eating only the M&Ms off the top of the cookie, in one piercing bite after another.

"Of course I would like it. Travel. Culture. Adventure ..." I was pointedly pulling each of my fingers down hoping my alleged certainty made him understand. Why didn't he get it? *What was I missing?*

"I'm just not sure that it's a good place for you to do any adventuring. And why Venezuela? You don't even speak Spanish. Uhhh, we could go to the Grand Canyon instead?" Insult after insult, my heart began beating its infamous drum of self-pity and doubt. I was awaiting that innate head-cock of pathetic sympathy to turn out on his face. *Don't you dare.*

Everything that Wes had given me in the sense of capabilities and effort was waiting in standing water during a lightning storm. The pure voltage of his implications far exceeded any couple's quarrel and any personal argument we had ever had. It was just one single, devastating lightning strike, as there was no storm nor even a cloud in that extended forecast.

Both in tone and deliverance, Wes' words sent my cerebrum straight back to that squishy slot in the part of your skull that is reserved only for those extremely defining, yet ravaging life experiences. That slot holds bits of hurt like your very first best friend's feelings on the playground, and that one time you yelled at your mom with such disgusting passion because you knew she'd still love you anyway. Synapses struck against the squishy mush to reveal a particular moment in my memory that felt so similar ...

I had been in search of a job for months. This small, little college town made for quite the difficult place to secure a job, any job. Luckily for me, I was virtually willing to do anything and do work for just about anyone. With an ever-growing geriatric population near campus (which I will still never fully understand), there was, too, an ever-growing abundance of nursing homes. What a perfect opportunity! I was studying biology with a sliver of hope that somebody would soon realize that all of my experience in the hospital in recent years should grant me an honorary medical license. Oh, and look: BIOOOOOLOGY. I was definitely a well-planned and optimistic college student.

With all of those courses in anatomy and chemistry, those old people caretakers were sure to hire me. And with that class-room confidence, I filled out the single-page application with the most professional-looking pen I could find in my polka-dotted pencil bag. Double check, triple check ... experience ... blah blah ... schooling. Done.

I was so sure of this job that I drove the application over to the nursing home myself, tying back my somewhat neglected, now chestnut-colored locks in a neat bow and throwing on the least wrinkled, blue buttoned-down blouse I could find off the floor. The blue matched my eyes and I thought for sure they were going to compliment me on that just after they had shaken my hand in a congratulatory fashion of both acceptance and approval of everything in existence.

When the time came for the handshake, somewhere just after the *thank yous* for coming in person and the remarks about my decent resume, there was a pause.

"Exactly *how* do you expect to do this job?" the muted, straight-pressed green scrubs seemed to asked with a shuttering emphasis on the word "how." The charge nurse, and owner of scrubs, looked puzzled.

"Pardon?" My voice cracked.

"I mean, child, it's not like you can carry *our* patients. You need to be able to carry our patients and push them in their own wheelchairs ..." Her voice trailed off, most likely hopeful that she wouldn't have to crush my spirit any more with her words. She tried desperately not to look at my wheelchair in front of her, so much so that I felt the potency of it.

Sometimes when you are presented with something new, it can be so far from your realm and scope of understanding that it just simply doesn't compute at all. The circuits were certainly firing here, but there was no proper instrument to receive them. I had completely shut down. Mostly a bouquet of fear, lack of understanding, utter devastation, and some delicately accented baby's breath. I had no idea how I was supposed to respond to such an offering.

I had always tried to believe that I could do anything. Isn't that what you are taught in school and colorful public service announcements? Now, all that I had was this abysmal bouquet of defeat to hand back to the woman who had just single-handedly shattered my own image of myself in a matter of seconds.

"Thank you for your time." My voice shook from false highs to sorrow-filled lows, and I clenched my teeth to try to hold everything in as I made my way back to my car. I had parked nearly two blocks away in the conscious effort to not take any spaces away from the nursing home inhabitants that I was soon to become friends with, or so I had unfathomably once believed. Giant stains of salty sadness penetrated straight through my delicately chosen blouse, as I messily sopped my tears up with it.

The embarrassment soon caught up to me as I pushed harder and harder to my car, which was going to double as the rock in which I wanted to die under. *How did I actually think that I was going to do it after all? Why didn't I think about that first? Why am I so stupid?*

And then it hit me.

What else can't I do?

That last question in my reverie sent me back to Wes. He was now standing with his back strategically turned to me as he looked off his front porch into the dry colors of the August landscape. I blinked hard both to bring myself out of that memory, and to tie up any loose tears that wanted to fall out of my eyeballs.

"We don't have to talk about it now," I called out with a sigh rendered from the defeat of today and yesterday. That nursing home revelation had been so neatly tucked away in my memory. I had nearly forgotten it altogether. Or, so I had thought.

I needed to let this go for now. I needed to let this go forever. Perhaps I need to let Wes go, too.

Wes, and his stupid overalls, never looked the same to me ever again.

diet coke culture

ALTHOUGH IT WAS SUPPOSED TO BE VENEZUELA, it wasn't. It was Paraguay. *That'll do too, I suppose.* Usually, the destination isn't the most important part of your adventure anyway.

The smaller, landlocked South American country of Paraguay had never been at the top of my list of places to visit. In fact, it had never even been on any of my lists whatsoever. Yet, I was on a plane in desperation to hold on to the only healthy romantic relationship I had ever thought I had. I wasn't about to admit it, but I was terrified.

I had boasted about traveling like this for years, and I thought I was tough enough. But maybe I wasn't. Looking out of the perfect oval-shaped window of the smallest plane I had never wished to travel in, my stomach ached in worry. The plane had just landed, and the crew still didn't know what to do with me.

I was just hopeful that they wouldn't lose or damage my wheel-chair since they took it from me and put it somewhere out of my view right before take-off.

"Silla ruedas?" I asked as I managed to cut-and-paste the little Spanish I knew.

"¿Puedes caminar? ¿Solo un poco?" No. No, I certainly could not walk, not even for a little bit. Not when we first boarded the plane and still not now. *What do these people expect?*

When that tiny plane's door opened, I suddenly understood. A tremendous metal staircase placed in front of the door. No other way out.

My terror leached out of my face, no doubt. The pilot began his creaky metal descent, as we caught eyes. I tried desperately to wipe away my look of horror, to no avail. After a brief, auction-esque Spanish exchange with the flight crew, the pilot came back up and approached me. He smiled and uttered something of which I understood none of. I smiled, too, hoping it was the correct answer to his question.

The next thing I knew, he was carrying me in both arms, like a child. He carried me straight out of the airplane and down the flight of stairs. I didn't realize it quite then, but his unintentional embrace was exactly what I needed to get off that plane.

Wes had, in the same manner a kindergarten show-off declares his love for never-climbed monkey bars, joined the Peace Corps and been sent rather expeditiously to the center of South America in hopes of fixing everything in the world. Everything, that was, except for our relationship.

He had been gone for months, and this was our first chance at reuniting, barring awkward half-emails and jumbled text messages at all hours of the day. It was my final Spring Break from my, finally, final year of college. I wanted so desperately to be with him and for things to be the same. I also wanted so desperately to be a whimsical traveler—that pack-my-under-wear-and-go sort of a gal.

Wes greeted me, almost nonchalantly, at the baggage carousel, where I had clearly packed more than just underwear. Our embrace felt so different from what I remembered. But I was relieved for the familiar face and the chance for adventure with him.

Both surprisingly and naturally, I loved Paraguay instantly. Something so remarkable about the people and the set-in-stone culture excited my soul like none other. I hadn't been out of the country much at all, especially since being born in a family where Dad was afraid of airplanes. I made it all the way to college being able to count the number of times I had been on a plane on two fingers.

The Paraguayans were curious and welcoming in a you-have-blondish-hair-and-blue-eyes sort of way. Everyone wanted to either touch me and my wheelchair or shift to the other side of the street to avoid me altogether. However, because my save-the-world boyfriend was placed by the Peace Corps, they had plopped him in a small village about one hundred miles outside of this swarming capital city, Asunción.

From Asunción, we took a bumpy, eight-hour, stop-and-go school bus ride sure to challenge anyone's patience and tailbone. Once out of the city and in the comforts of a small village on the hem of a powdered reddish dirt road, I threw my bags down on a small cot designated for me and apparently a larger-than-life, unwavering toad.

The family who housed Wes was composed of a single pillowy-proportioned mother, who wore more than the weight of a failed marriage and caregiver to her elderly, abrasive father. Her six-year-old mischievous sidekick, who taunted me from the start, fell almost unnoticed in her shadow at first. They were all remarkably warm in receiving my blondish, foreign quirks and immediately motioned me out to the back of the house. Wes and the entire family followed closely behind. They were all watching me. I could feel it.

The five of us sat around in a circle and prepared to connect over old traditions and new company. Dirt-colored chickens roamed too close and needed a good old swat from the mama, which allowed me to further take in the moment and this apparent ritual, as the rest of my company was squawkingly distracted. I watched intently and in silence, seeing as I was the only one who could not communicate in either Spanish or the native language, Guarani.

The clear leader of the family wasn't actually that pillowy mama, although I'm certain onlookers would challenge me on that. It was so obvious to me that it was really her father—Taitaguasu.

With all eyes on me, Taitaguasu uncovered a wooden cup— out of where I would never be quite sure—and a metal straw as its counterpart. Motioning behind me, Taitaguasu guided another elderly man to our circle, a very old friend of his, from what I could discern through body language. The two were two beings cut from similar stone. They did not smile at one another, yet their love for each other was evident to me.

Taitaguasu's friend donned a thermos jug with colors that indicated to me it was either manufactured somewhere off in the distance of the late '70s, or just ungodly filthy, or both. The friend, with a notion of methodology and monotony, pulled a clear plastic bag with dried vegetation, the only window from his oversized pockets. He bounced the bag on his knee to shake up its contents and prepare it for departure. I was pretty sure my face made it perfectly clear that I certainly did not travel across countries to do some drugs with an old man and friend, his daughter, and her exasperating son—even if it was for Wes.

In true form, my face told the whole story that was made possible by the dancing synapses in my brain, which Wes was very accustomed to me and that natural indication. He assured me we were not about to partake in anything scandalous, although he did choose to put a certain disclaimer on it: "What he is making is a tea drink, yerba mate. It is a native drink that the locals share anywhere and everywhere. In fact, I think that this drink is probably responsible for nothing ever getting done around here." Wes, being a natural teacher, took that opportunity to express that natural tone too. Usually enamored, I was more annoyed by his tone. It felt so condescending to me. It was such a change in taste that I was not prepared for.

Regardless of this altered flavor, I kept listening without making a sound. I figured they couldn't understand me or my English, but I still didn't want to risk offending anyone, especially that aggressive and agitated Taitaguasu displaying rotten teeth and an even more rotten demeanor.

"See that cup? It's called a *guampa*. The straw has a sifter at the end, and it is called a *bombilla*. We drink this stuff all the time. I think you'll really like it, but be careful—the water is not filtered." Wes was always so casual in his teacher tone, which was probably one of the reasons that I first fell for him. He couldn't help but be casually cool yet informative. He was a natural at it, and typically, did so with little condescendence. But today was different.

When I first met Wes, he tried to play it very cool and mature when offering up information about muscle contractions and nerve impulses as my teacher, full knowing that we were only months apart in age. I knew better. I saw right through him, his bushy chocolate, facial-hair-makes-you-look-older beard, and his forced maturity from the very start.

I fondly remember the first day that I ever laid my gaze on him in class. As he dismissed us all after a brief synopsis of things to come in lab, I quickly called my best friend, Faye, and told her that I was in love.

Now, being a hopeless, yet hapless, romantic for my entire life, Faye was neither surprised nor deterred by my proclamation. I continued by exclaiming that he was terribly short, had ears that quite possibly could be used for spontaneous flight, teeth that resembled pearly corn kernels, and thick curly black hair that stood on end.

"I have no idea why. I just know I am in love." That was the first and nearly last time I had ever been so sure of my heart.

Those events that drew us together three years prior also led us to that moment outside that little Paraguayan hut, preparing to drink some ritual mate. It was less about the actual hydration of the drink or even about the bitter, yet tantalizing, tasteful scent.

I learned it was more about the actual process of the drink, in terms of the preparation and sharing of it. Families, friends, coworkers, and even strangers like myself came together in Paraguay for a moment of sharing the *guampa* with each other. This was time to forget about all woes and concerns for the world. Yet, strangely, I don't think there is even a word for "cheers!" in Guarani. Perhaps there is a clear reason for it. They weren't drinking for that.

When it became my turn, I honed in on Wes' final warning: *the water wasn't filtered.* The last thing that I needed was to ingest an intestinal parasite here in this little village with no handicapped access, let alone a true bathroom in sight. So, I did the best that I could. I took the wooden cup graciously from Taitaguasu, who smiled for the first time a gapped and bleeding-gum sort of a smile. The cup was much colder than I suspected. *Where did these folks get ice, anyway?* As my lips tightened over the metal straw, the coolness of the yerba pushed upward into my mouth in one exuberant motion. Yes, I liked it!

It was tea, and it was cold, but I didn't want to risk becoming a host to any sort of native nematode, so I faked the rest. I slurped some air and smiled at the family, who all smiled back. We were now all friends. I had drunk from their prized *guampa*, reserved for special guests, and graciously waved on the cup to the mama now seated next to me. No matter that I couldn't tell them with my words, I was hoping my smile could share my respect with them all.

In remembering this event, I can't help but think of my family and its own particular and peculiar traditions and rituals. One startling realization was that we were not very far off from that family living in that dusted floor hut in the middle of South America.

My family was composed of a soft, yet clearance-itemed, plastic picture frame of kinship. In that frame held the portrait of my mother and father, who grew to loathe one another in equal fashion, but you would never tell by the picture though. Nearer the bottom were me and my younger, most-impressionable sister, who decided very early on to be the embodiment of the exact contrary to me. We always loved each other because we were family, and the permanence and pressure of our own unspoken traditions united us.

Every family has them, whether intentional or not. Those traditions that carry you through honey-baked hams at Christmastime or gin rummy on New Year's Eve. They are paramount to all familial culture. It doesn't matter if it is a small blondish family plopped in the middle of the United States, or a small brownish family in the middle of South America. Those traditions exist and continue as a lifeline of sorts.

Although extremely far away from the *guampas* and *bombillas* of Paraguayan delight, my family had our own, equally bizarre and insisting practices. Who's to say ours was better or worse than others? On the one hand, they rarely included bleeding gums and swapping straws, but consequentially they rarely included basic conversation either.

My mother, in particular, was completely fascinated by the existence of Diet Coke. For as long as I can remember, there was a Diet Coke in her hand—or in her purse when she was attempting to be more refined for the public eye. Back then, I didn't quite realize it, but it was those little things that I witnessed as a child that grew to have an immense impact on every part of me.

Still to this day, there isn't a family event without a Diet Coke. I have learned to accept said Aspartame-iferous, fizzy beverage without hesitation. There was no way to refuse the love that was implied in the Diet Coke. For those colors of glossy red and metallic white exude the purest emotions of love and family, don't they?

About a billion years too late, my mom and dad finally parted ways, but not tradition. It didn't matter if I was visiting Mom in her townhome strategically positioned just feet away from the very house we grew up in, or Dad, who did his best to erase that home altogether. The Diet Coke flowed freely and lovingly from both establishments, and I accepted it without the slightest thought or remorse from either.

That Diet Coke became the ultimate symbol of my family dynamic. It is full of fake, sugar-free, sweetness but widely loved anyway. It isn't really good for you—you won't let your kids drink it, right? But you can handle it, even with its Surgeon General's Warning. I suppose one could say that I hold a little tension for that particular soft drink and the ranks it held in my family.

The Paraguayans used their drink to become a way of bonding with one another over the conversation of the day, political rants, and tales passed down from the way things were. We utilized the Diet Coke as a way to replace the entire need for conversation itself.

That lack of communication among the members in my family was both equally appalling and astonishing. To actually exchange glimpses of feelings with words was simply out of the question, even in the early days after my accident, where emotions ran quite high. There was still little to be said ... about anything. Ever.

This family dynamic became most unfortunate when I got into my accident. People say that true colors are tested and brought to light under significant moments of pain and trauma. This was undoubtedly true and, after my accident, it was extremely safe to say that the colors of my family bled into a muddled and putrid brown. Poop brown. Or maybe throw-up brown. Either way, it was a brown color no one wanted painted on their walls.

Sometimes it is hard for me to understand what my family went through that night, or those months afterward, or even today.

Perhaps it is because *they* never told *me*.

My quick response when people ask about how my family dealt with my accident was that it was hardest on them, and I was the lucky one to be in the position that I was in. I have always felt this because I saw how it manifested differently in each one of them, and the pain was deep. Despite having used this catch-phrase dozens of times over the years, it is clearly obvious to me that no one actually understood what was meant by it. Most times, people would reply with a simple, head-cocked nod. That pity nod followed me everywhere.

The accident happened to *me*. The paralysis happened to *me*. The death of my boyfriend happened to *me*. People would nod mostly when they didn't know what to say. Very few people have ever walked, or wheeled in this instance, in shoes like mine. It really isn't so bad. I'm telling you the truth.

Put all of the things in a sealed-up mason jar and move on. The things that are icky and sticky and nod-worthy. You look through the thick glass every once in a while, but they are like lightning bugs you've caught on a warm summer's night. They stay in the jar because you want them to stay. You look at them when you want, but eventually, unless you let them go, they will probably die in there.

I couldn't live unless I put those things and memories away. I had to move past them.

It's one thing for me to say as the person who this all happened to. But it is quite another thing, I imagine, when it all happens to someone you love. Not my mom, nor dad, nor even little Abby would ever recover from it all.

Watching a loved one struggle is one of the cruelest concepts that the world could claim. Feeling helpless for the person in pain. It is human nature to want to help, and so utterly dismantling when you can't act on such an innate desire. I only learned this in my adulthood, and never quite understood my own burden of myself when I was younger.

I actually can't blame my accident or the months it took me to heal, or even that Diet Coke communication strategy wholly. But there was something else, something like an invisible strangler fig surrounding my family. It held my family tightly and wholly.

For years, well before my accident, I noticed things every so often. Sometimes my dad would sleep on the couch. Sometimes my mom would seem lost, even in the middle of *our* house. Sometimes my dad would ignore everyone, even in the same room. Sometimes my mom would look sad.

That shifty fig had been unintentionally planted several years before my spine shattered, and my family's world followed quickly behind. If it wasn't enough to have my family fall apart on its own, we had to expedite the process with my stupid accident. I know it's not my fault. Sometimes it's hard to continue to tell myself that. I know things wouldn't have been okay or normal otherwise. I really do. Damned fig tree.

When Wes dropped me off, we shared a goodbye of mate at the airport prior to boarding my plane.

The airplane door closed and flight attendants spoke in twirly tongues that I didn't quite understand. I was leaving Paraguay and felt much different from when I had arrived. Somehow, none of it felt that surprising. My promptly welling eyes scanned around at the seats of families and preoccupied travelers. The flight attendant caught my watering eyes and asked if I needed anything, in her half-English, half-Spanish smiling attempt.

"I'll have a Diet Coke."

dear diary

"**YOU CAN JUST SET THEM OVER THERE**, by the other ones," I said pointing toward a generous pile of carefully taped-up boxes with labels like "Gma's Stuff" and "Random Office Supplies." You would think that by now that I would have this moving thing down to an art. But, alas, it was always one of those struggles that I wanted to blame on my wheelchair and also not blame at the same time. Truth be told, I would be terrible at packing and moving no matter what. The wheelchair didn't play a role, but it took the blame anyway. I just opened a box that held a dead potted plant, a tube of chapstick, and a couple of dusty books. That was all there was in the box. Pathetic. I had to blame something.

As soon as I graduated high school, I began jumping around from apartment to apartment, securing myself monthly leases when I could take advantage of them. I didn't want to ever go back to that basement apartment in my parent's broken household. Even the Christmas boxes were collecting dust there.

I moved back and forth from college town to my hometown seemingly out of necessity, but I also think I partly did it to create some controlled chaos in my life. My first apartment I signed the lease for when I was eighteen. It was such a desolate old building. But it was absolutely perfect for a desolate teenage me. In fact, the management had to remove all the doors and doorframes inside of it just so that I could even squeeze through to the other rooms. Even the bathroom had nothing more than a sliding screen screwed into the side of the wall where the doorframe used to be.

That apartment was desperate. I was desperate. It was a beautiful marriage of folly and adventure. I fought so hard at that young age, just to have some independence, or so I thought. Looking back, though, I may have gone a bit overboard in that struggle to prove my independence. However, I've never lost an ounce of stubbornness or a bit of self-sacrifice over the years. I'd do it all again in a heartbeat.

If I really wanted to break free from the things that could have held me back from being put in this wheelchair, I needed to figure it out on my own. It also helped, perhaps, that my family was tearing apart at the seams. I couldn't find any comfort or stability among any of them anymore.

I suppose that had led me to moving, yet again. Opening some of the cryptically written labeled boxes, I started finding things that never got quite unpacked from previous, tinier apartments. It was all packed in crumpled newspapers from years that had since come and gone.

Resting and wiping my hand across an unassuming notebook from the box labeled "Random Office Supplies," I immediately felt an emotion that I hadn't expected nor felt in quite some time. It was an immediate game of tug-a-war between a happy, reminiscent version of myself versus another younger me that rocked quietly in the corner with fear.

I had just found my old diary.

I flipped open to one of the first entries and softly read it, although I tried so hard not to. One eye had closed unknowingly, almost in an attempt to guard me, as I read the first page.

MARCH 29, 1994

What is in that bottle? I threw away everything. I think? It's kind of scaring me. All the pills that I could find, but she still is acting funny. I cleaned out the entire medicine cabinet, I don't even know what half of that stuff is. I threw them all over the fence. I don't want to do anything wrong. I just know that I can't tell Dad. I know I probably should, I'm only 13 after all … but I don't know what he will do. He doesn't really talk that much.

Swallowing hard, I thumbed past a couple more pages. Taking a deep breath inward, I read on.

NOVEMBER 11, 1995

I know Rebecca and Allie don't get it. What should I tell them? I just don't want to have them spend the night at my house anymore. Last time was a mess. I can't believe that Mom did that. There was no way for me to pretend to them that my mom was okay. It's so embarrassing. Ugh. She sat on the floor with her back to the TV telling us that she was watching TV! Seriously! She is so embarrassing. I can't even figure it out. She's fine during the day, but just gets that funny look in her face at night. It must be sleeping pills. Maybe I should go through the medicine cabinet again. Maybe she hides it somewhere else. That face that she makes. It's like she doesn't even look like herself. Her eyes are cold and gray. She looks like someone mean. Someone I don't know.

I stopped reading with an innate, and unintentional hard exhale. I must have been holding my breath while I was reading. Why did I save this? What did I want to do with this? *Why am I still reading?*

JANUARY 4, 1996

We're out of grape jelly again and I know Abby is only going to eat grape jelly. She's going to have a cow, but she had better be okay with strawberry. She's just going to have to be. I hate making lunches. I hate hiding it from everyone. I hate putting Mom to bed, but I hate it more when she chases me.

I wish she could make Abby's stupid sandwich. I wish she could be normal again. I wish I could figure out what was wrong with her. I wish the nighttime wouldn't come.

I don't think that she is sick—otherwise maybe I'd tell Dad. Or maybe not. I'm not sure Dad would do anything anyways. I hope he's okay with strawberry jelly too. I'm so tired. I need to go to bed, I have morning swim practice .... ugh. Sometimes I just wish I'd break my leg or something so I didn't have to go to practice. I probably shouldn't think like that. But, I'm just so tired.

MAY 22, 1996

Tonight, Dad found out. I tried really hard not to go upstairs. I really did. I kinda did.

I ran through the family room and up to the kitchen. I ran circles around the kitchen into the dining room. Then I did it. She just wouldn't stop. I didn't know what else to do. I guess I was scared. Maybe I did it on purpose. Maybe I wanted him to find out.

I ran upstairs. I guess I knew that it would wake Dad. Right then I wanted it to wake him. Was that selfish of me?

Anyway, I ran upstairs straight to my room and slammed the door right on her funny-looking face. Don't tell anyone, but it sorta felt good. It felt like something I've wanted to do for a long time now. I stayed behind my door the whole time. It felt good to be able to hide from her for once. I think I even closed my eyes. That's silly, I know.

There was a little fight, but less than I thought it would be. I moved to my closet, to continue my moment of hiding. I guess it was so comfortable, I fell asleep. The next morning Mom couldn't understand why I was asleep in my closet.

She never remembered any of it. Nothing. But I knew that Dad would.

JUNE 1, 1996

I was so worried that Dad would find out about Mom, but once he did, I actually felt like I could breathe better. Is that weird? I slept really well and dreamed of swimming in a river that led into a big sea where I found some mermaids who wanted to brush my hair. It felt so good. They were so beautiful and loving. I wish I could go back to sleep and get back to that dream.

Dad came into my room this morning, which was also strange because I can't remember the last time that he was even in here. He even sat down on my futon! He asked me what we were going to do about Mom. He asked me!

What?! I finally thought that maybe this would get fixed because now Dad knew, but now he wanted ME to help HIM? I don't even think I said anything to him. I tried, but nothing came out. I just kept thinking about those mermaids brushing my hair.

AUGUST 18, 1996

Today was my birthday. My sixteenth birthday. I was really excited to go to the pool with Rebecca, and Allie, and Rob (of course) but then I got in trouble. I don't even know what I did. Mom just started yelling at me, and it was so weird because she actually looked a lot like she does at night. Maybe she's getting worse? I can't really tell, but why hasn't Dad done anything about it?

I spent most of this stupid day walking around the neighborhood without any shoes on. I just ran out of the house, and as my brain was telling me to stop and grab my swimsuit and some breakfast, I just ran anyways. I ran out of the garage in bare feet and didn't even look back at her.

Maybe I should have grabbed Abby too. Ugh. Hopefully she'll go play dollhouse with her friend in the cul-de-sac. What a stupid birthday. I'm not really sure if I am supposed to be mad or just really, really sad today. I wonder what normal sixteen-year-olds do on their birthday?

At this point, the movers had left, and this white-walled and bare apartment lingered all around me. I picked up the diary off of my lap and fanned forward a few pages. Getting increasingly more emotional, I just couldn't read it all.

Just then, one handwritten date struck me—I read aloud, "February 19, 1997." It was as though I expected those blank walls to express some sort of concern for that.

That date was the first entry I had made after my accident.

I was not even twenty days out of it. I didn't remember writing in my diary that soon, but I am sure I needed to.

FEBRUARY 19, 1997

Last night was really, really scary. For some reason, I am so afraid to breathe on my own. This ventilator machine has been helping me breathe for the last couple weeks and everyone is sure that I can do it on my own, but it is so scary. All the humming, it's so loud.

Why am I so scared?

This ventilator machine is keeping me alive.

The tubing is all a very pretty blue color, which I think was done on purpose in order to hide how scary the stupid thing actually is. It's really big. The tubing connects the air from the machine directly into a hole in my throat—which is actually the grossest thing that I can think of right now. Sometimes the tubing pops away from the plastic piece on the front of my throat. It makes a really loud dinging noise, so people have to rush to reconnect it. Mostly they get there before I really freak out. But last night, Mom didn't even wake up.

Mom and Dad have been taking turns sleeping in the chair next to my hospital bed, and it was Mom's turn and I wish it wasn't. She didn't wake up to the beeping and alarms of the machine. I couldn't breathe or speak because of the way the tube thing works. Everything in my body was getting tight and tired. I could see little sparkles through my eyes, it was bad and I had to do something because Mom clearly wasn't going to. I was so dizzy but managed to grab a little stuffed animal crab resting near my arm and threw it as hard as I could out the door into the hospital hallway. Then I threw the purple duck, or is it a platypus? Then a ladybug and a puppy, but both of them fell short. I should have played softball more and not given up so easily. Dad would have stayed more if I played softball.

Finally, one of the stuffed animal slingshots did the trick and several nurses came storming in and reconnected me and my tubes. They calmed me down and made me feel much better and even safe. I was crying, and trying so hard not to. I don't really let them see me cry.

They like me for that, I think? I want to be strong and brave for them, for the nurses.

Mom slept through the whole thing.

Yesterday Shawn and some other friends came to visit me. It was nice to see him because he has no idea how to handle really scary stuff, like being in the hospital, so he just laughs and tells me about stupid stuff at school.

It was a good break, until he got very still and serious once everyone stepped out of the room to get some hot cocoa. Shawn's face turned in a way that I had never seen before. I was already lying in a hospital bed, half naked, and hooked up to all sorts of tubes and machines. What could he possibly say?

He told me with a whisper in his throat that he thought that he needed to tell me something about my mom.

He told me that she smelled like alcohol. ALCOHOL.

FEBRUARY 23, 1997

It was several days later for me to sit with those syllables in my throat: al-co-hol. Finally, I phoned Shawn and asked him for a visit. Obviously, he said that he'd be right over. He was a good friend and I know that he feels really badly about everything. He just lost his best friend, Jeremy, and now has to tell the half-naked hospital girl about her alcoholic mother. *Geez*.

He was that teddy bear sort of guy that had a heart for everyone, because he never knew to leave any for himself. And in many ways because of that, he was also the only one to be able to recognize what was going on with my mom.

Once he arrived, I had already made up the plan. Mom had left to give us some time to "catch up" ... whatever that means. I knew that she'd buy it though. She really goes along with anything these days. You'd think that I'd love the fact that she would just give into me for any reason right now, but in all reality—honestly—I just want her to be a mom.

I want a mom to tell me, "NO!" when I'm being a bossy teenager or when I want that color-changing tee-shirt that everyone who's popular wears. Where is *that* mom hiding? Where did she go?

Anyway, Shawn and I were left alone, so he handed me her purse. 1 ...2 ...3 ...little bottles of *SOMETHING*. All I could do was put them back and shove the purse right at Shawn's chest. He left immediately. He knew. He knew I needed some time.

Sitting in my new apartment, reading my own words, some of which I had forgotten, some I wish I had, I wondered why I had to write all this down. *Did I really have to write it? Did it cross anyone else's hands in my journey from hospital to home?* I shuffled past a few more pages.

MAY 27, 1997

It was scary being home. I never thought that the hospital would feel so comfortable to me, but for some reason it began to feel like the only comfort I had. It felt safe and uncomplicated. I feel like inside those walls I could never really get hurt, I didn't have to face anyone if I didn't want to, and I could keep hiding from everything that had happened. I never had to really think about this stupid wheelchair before. That sounds stupid, but in the hospital, EVERYONE had a wheelchair so I didn't really have to think about mine.

My parents were trying, sort of. They spent a lot of money making my own apartment down-stairs. Everyone loves it, and I pretend to love it. I can't really hear what's going on upstairs from way down here.

Mom comes down once a day for the laundry. I wish she would just leave me alone. I can never really tell when she is going to be okay and when she isn't.

Today was a mess. I am not even sure what I did, but she was so mad. So mad. She kept yelling from at the top of the staircase, I couldn't even understand her, she was just so mad.

I had moved myself onto my bed just to get out of my chair for a bit, just like they had taught me to do in the hospital. Bad idea, hospital folks. When you get out of your chair, you can lose the chair and all your freedom.

Before I knew it, Mom was marching big steps down the stairs into my dungeon "apartment." I guess it was my fault. I started yelling back, because I didn't really know why she was mad in the first place. I think everyone does that, right? Everyone starts yelling when they are getting yelled at or at least they do in my house. But I guess it is still my fault.

Anyway, she started really acting scary. She came straight to me and grabbed me at my wrists flat down at my bed. I guess she thought that she could yell at me better if I wasn't moving. I couldn't do anything. I was stuck under her weight and anger.

When she was done with the yelling, she turned quickly around like she was going to storm off, but must have been caught by my chair. The wheel got caught at her leg. It almost made me laugh, if I wasn't so scared. She was mad at my wheelchair?

The look she gave my wheelchair was unforgettable. Then, she took my chair away from me. She took it up the stairs, struggling the whole way with it.

So, here I am, stuck on my bed. I hate her. I hate this.

I am still crying.

It's been three hours.

Cringing, I flipped past some more pages. The pages were warm and soft between my fingers. The edges had changed and worn because of time, yet the content inside had been left unscathed by any time or anything at all. Those words were just as fresh as the day they were written.

Those memories had been left untouched in my brain as well. I think it was all too much for me to take, really, on top of relearning how to be a normal teenager in a wheelchair. Instead of being overwhelmed, my brain did its due diligence and tucked it all away somewhere. Those memories were actually intact, just like the pages of the diary.

JANUARY 10, 2000

I'm really glad to be away at college. I've met some cool people and I really feel like I am finally starting to figure things out for myself. But I also know that—on some level—I am terribly stuck and I am afraid I may be stuck for good.

I am constantly bombarded with thoughts of Abby and everyone else back home. I constantly feel guilty and I just know that my grades are suffering.

I mean, I guess I can't blame that solely on my family. I just always feel so distracted and no one totally understands. I leave for a few hours to drive the two-hours it takes to get back just to take Abby to choir practice. Usually, I don't tell my roommates what I am doing because I think they will think that I am ridiculous. I just tell them that I am going to go to the movies with some friends they don't know.

They are probably pissed that I don't invite them too, but whatever.

I tend to tread really lightly with my new friends—no one really knows me that well. I think I am too scared to lose the few friends I've made.

These friends, they never even knew me when I could walk. Isn't that strange? They only know me in my wheelchair. Does that make a difference? Is it better? Worse? I guess this is why I am so scared. Would I have been friends with me now?

MARCH 30, 2000

Last night I checked myself into the hospital for the first time ever. It was actually pretty easy to do. But Eve and I had to cut our Spring Break plans in Las Vegas short because of this stupid 103°F fever that I got yesterday. We had plans to go to Cirque du Soleil, which I was definitely not going to miss, so I did my best to play it off until I started convulsing so badly that Eve knew it was time to drive home. Luckily for me, she drives like a bat out of hell drinking an energy drink even in a normal circumstance. She got us home to campus in record-time.

Eve is awesome. She is so kind and free-spirited. I wish I could be just like her. She has such a striking beauty and innocence about her—I bet that is what gets her into trouble. She is the baby of her family, and used to getting away with things.

We met in French class last year. She chose me as her partner—me?! We were instant friends as there was nothing you couldn't like about her. Her love of people and animals made you feel like you were making the world a better place just knowing her. And then she would park in a tow-away zone and convince you that it was okay. She is my first real friend here, I think.

Anyway, we drove straight to Eve's house where we dropped her off and I slid over to the driver's seat to make my way to the hospital. I have an infection in my skin. I'm stuck in the hospital. Alone. But I don't really want to tell anyone either.

But then I got calls on my cell phone from "Home" several times in a row today. I didn't want to answer because I knew that they'd either hear the beeping IV machine next to me or they'd tell I was lying though my voice, or both. But after the twelfth-ish time, I picked up.

Mom had two seizures at work and was put in the hospital.

I held back any and every emotion I had as Abby spoke to me. She spoke to me with such frankness in her own voice that every word stung as it echoed through my hospital walls. I couldn't tell her that I was in the hospital too, that would be too much. We were both in the hospital, ugh. Of course we were.

APRIL 18, 2000

It's been a few weeks that Mom's been at Charter Valley Hope. What a dumb name. Hope for what? The doctors keep saying that she is doing really well, but I think that she is acting like a cartoon character. They didn't know her before this, so how can they be so sure. She thinks that she is recovering from a disease—a disease! The doctors say that's okay.

DIS-EASE ... ya, me too.

Her main doctor gave me an assignment, as if I don't have enough already. I'm trying to juggle Organic Chemistry and Cell Biology—what am I, an idiot?! Right now, I'm sitting here, supposed to be studying for this exam, but instead I'm writing in this stupid diary. Who am I even writing to? Whoever it is, I want to tell you that my fake smile hurts my cheeks. I'm TIRED. I'm tired and I'm over it.

So much for studying. I've got to work on this "assignment" for the doctors—well, I guess for my mom. I have to write Mom a letter. I am supposed to be able to tell her everything that I would ever want to, or wanted to, or whatever. I'm supposed to tell her how I felt or how I feel—are those the same things right now? I am not even sure where to start.

Maybe tomorrow. Right now, I'd rather learn about molecular bonding, or mass suicide, or even poaching endangered baby seals. Anything other than write that letter.

~~DEAR MOM,~~
~~I have never been so mad in my life. YOU haven't~~
~~been there for me. You don't even know what I am~~
~~doing at school or what my apartment looks like.~~
~~I live in that apartment because I don't want to be~~
~~near you. Do you even know that I went to Paris?~~
~~Do you remember all those nights~~

~~DEAR MOM,~~
~~I hate what you have done to me. I hate what~~
~~you have done to all of us. You have no idea because~~
~~you can't even remember ANY of it~~

MOM,
I am sorry that this has happened to you. I hope that you are getting well and I hope that you will be able to take care of yourself better. We all miss you and want everything to be okay again.
Love,
me

PART
TWO

recipe for my acceptance of your acceptance of accepting me

PREP TIME: A brief flicker in time, to seemingly none at all
TOTAL TIME: If you're lucky, every single time
SERVINGS: That's up to you

INGREDIENTS

3-1/4 C patience, sifted
2 C humility, beaten thoroughly
2 T understanding
2 T pure cane love
2 People, interacting as one for a moment
1 t freshly picked stalk of wisdom
1 dash of stubbornness to taste
(optional—the willingness to learn and grow)

DIRECTIONS

1. Turn that oven in your mindset to a temperature that you are comfortable enough with to remain open to opportunity and wisdom. Always proceed with caution, however, because even in the most unexpected and unlikely of sources, you may reach uncomfortable temperatures rather quickly.

2. Add 2 cups of humility and remember that the qualities of a child's mind are the perfect compilation of inquisition and simplicity. (You may even need to increase quantities at higher altitudes.)

   Don't hesitate to smile at that child who became instantly fascinated by your "*stroller*" and the fact that it is much, much larger than theirs. It may be just that that child sees you for you, with no preconceived notion of your capabilities or lack therein. That "stroller" isn't you—it's that thing that helps you get around just like that sweet child. You need it for movement, but it is certainly not you. There is no need for you to accept the mother's apology, even though she really seemed as she needed you to.

3. In a separate bowl, add all the dry ingredients with an electric mixer, if possible.

   When mixing together a wheelchair wheel and a bra, you might find some difficulty—but keep mixing until both are taut and tangled. Going unnoticed until you leave your dorm room, that mixture is now just right. You can then recognize any offered help as something good and even necessary. Any embarrassment of the situation is a roadblock emotion, one that will clearly deny access to the most crucial parts of learning and yearning. Your experience will be a way that the universe can guide you further toward more important things.

It will add just a pinch of salt and sprinkle down upon you. Ever so slight, yet covering everything beneath. That salt is there to help prime everything in the pot.

NOTE: *The salt will not affect the overall taste of the completed dish.*

With something less than grace, but more than stupidity, that bra can end up wrapped in knots of wannabe pretzels around one's wheelchair wheels. This will cause them to tighten up so closely together that both will give out in one simple, exhausting display. Thus forcing wheel, chair, and user to all reevaluate their current recipe. Having the capabilities to have a bra wind its way around in the outside world, beyond the intimacy of where it is meant, could be extremely hazardous and ill-advised. Stop mixing immediately and let stand for 10 minutes.

When that doesn't work, and the last one on this planet to help you out of your pretzel-bra bind is your dorm resident assistant, you allow some help graciously and with praise of one's accidental role they just played. As this is truly an essential lesson in personal growth and willingness to let go and accept someone's help when it's offered. Red-faced embarrassment is truly fleeting. And, again, that salt won't affect the overall outcome.

4.   Understanding that sometimes you have to fold in both your own acceptance of the situation along with others' acceptance is when you will truly begin to start cooking. Combine wet ingredients to the dry.

My acceptance of being able to manage things at both a different rate and procedure has been one thing. But, realizing that it is also my need to take in that same acceptance that others have toward accepting me in *my* acceptance is another thing (and mouthful) entirely.

"*I'm okay, really. Yes, really. There are worse things than being in a wheelchair. Honestly, you don't have to feel bad for me. Oh no, please don't cry for me ... Oh, no. Oh, there's no need to pray for me either. Please get up. Have a nice day.*"

5.   In a separate, clear glass bowl, stir gently to not disturb and overload any one single ingredient on its own.

Having learned independence as a way of stabilization, then having those courteously around you literally rip that notion of independence straight from your hands could end quite badly—especially if one doesn't remember those original, separate ingredients from the start.

Independence can be gained from simple things like driving a car, owning a car, or even something far more taken for granted—getting out of a car.

Ripping one's wheelchair from their own palms as they place it strategically next to the opened car door, as they had thousands of times before, also rips away one's own autonomy and pride. However, there must be an acknowledged notion of help among the other, as to make sure the two mixtures don't curdle in utter disgust of one another. So, keep folding the two seemingly separate parts of acceptance together—your own and the others'. Eventually, you will have one completed recipe—but you must keep going until you get there.

RECIPE TIP: *Using a transparent bowl may be crucial in ultimately determining this mixing process.*

6. With the remaining 2 tablespoons of understanding, take the wisdom you've gained from the above steps and pour all of it graciously over the entire mixture. Repeat as necessary, for each batch can differ from the next. Some people aren't able to comprehend the power that lies in the perspective that can be gained when your eyes are truly open.

More than a dozen years later, in the same high school halls where I once swore my life was over, I came back as not a student, but a teacher instead.

Within my classroom walls buzzed lessons of mitosis and cell theory, but most importantly, radiated lessons of acceptance and courage, of determination and pride. However, every so often, you will encounter one that has missed the lesson entirely. "*I would never want to live if I had your life*" or "*Doesn't your life, like, completely suck?*" are surefire signs that the lesson was not taught, the recipe had not been followed correctly, and pretty soon you were going to have to start over again from scratch.

In this case, throw it all away and restart from the beginning, Step #1.

7. If your batter was successful, however, transfer your prepared acceptance into the bowl set out to rise and grow as it will over time.

   Take a deep breath before you react to a woman who spied you pulling into that sacred handicapped parking space. She had made it her mission to stand up for justice and get that stupid little teenager out of that reserved spot, obviously not designed for me. People who need those spots clearly couldn't be teenagers, not ever.

   The lack of air that would explain such things as why you had every right to park there, could keep the dough from rising. Do not give up though, even when not wanting to admit any of it and rather having the woman think only idiot kids would park there, not uneasy, deserving kids.

   I drove away in tears.

   RECIPE TIP: *Dough may need to rest longer than you would expect in order for it all to work and rise to its full potential.*

8. Optional: Top with sweetness and well-intended stranger, if desired, prior to baking. Understand that even though someone may not see you for you, they are trying. Accept the things that you get from the universe simply because you are different.

   With open arms and a large, toothy smile, accept the following: free bottles of champagne when your under-aged-self has been assigned to the back of the airplane (isn't that where all the popular fliers go?), high fives and encouragement to keep you going from across bike paths by overweight and sweaty men out for their half-a-mile ride, as well as being herded to the front of the line at the Louvre as the only French way of saying, "*Madam, we really just don't want you to sue us when you find out you cannot possibly ever have any hope at actually seeing the Venus de Samothrace up close.*"

9. Bake this together for a lifetime or longer, if needed. Sometimes the acceptance goes far beyond you and me to something else much more moving and complex. That something is not quite understood, nor will it ever. But never fear—that is exactly how it is all supposed to be.

goodnight grandma

"PLEASE TELL ME YOU'RE NOT AT THE MALL AGAIN?"
As Faye waited for a reply that was never meant to surface, she continued, "This will be the sixth time this week ... and it's only Tuesday."

"Uh-hu ..." my voice dropped off as if my soul was anchored by those words, or any words for that matter. As my best friend of nearly a decade, Faye knew that it was troublesome that I was at the mall at all, let alone repeatedly over the last few days. She was right.

Somehow, I seemed to always find myself at the mall when I was at my worst. I don't know how it always happened, and the execution was always hazy. But, nonetheless, there I was—again.

I'm not even sure how I arrived at the West Mills Mall that afternoon. *Did I really drive here? And park here too? It's going to be a delight to try to find my car.* Time seemed to have drifted away into a black hole of clearance sales and neatly folded cardigans. I must have been there for hours. *I should probably eat something—this week.*

I finally mustered up enough energy to assuredly lie to Faye and declare to her that I was fine, at which she reminded me, yet again, to let her know if I needed anything. I moaned and hung up the phone in a very definitive, sign language sort of manner. And, although I didn't let her know it, Faye's voice was so comforting. It was always comforting. Maybe that's just why I had clung to her as my best friend for so many years.

Her hair stood out in front of the world, as she often did, chanting and protesting the currently downtrodden. It was the same color as mine, but in a complete realm of its own. The way the strands twisted and whirled about, surrounding her softened face, offered quite a contrast. Sort of in the same way that she was. Faye was the most compassionate soul, with a rebellion underbelly. She wanted to help everything and everyone, but only do so if it could be done outside of the lines and out of that box. Right now, I didn't care about any lines or boxes, but I couldn't help but sigh a small relief as I hung up the phone.

At this point, I was nestled up between the mall's ketchup-stained trashcan and blue painted, metal bench, neither of which I felt any comfort. Everything seemed to move in slow motion. Children were running and playing, mothers were yelling and garment pulling, and fathers were wincing and wandering.

In those moments at the mall, I noticed everything that no one else bothered. I watched a young teen with her friends, wishing she were home with her overworked mother instead. I translucently saw a widower grab for a hand that was no longer there. I counted gumballs of every primary color, even the warped and cracked ones, because they deserved to be counted too. The fog in my eyes couldn't be mistaken for anything other than what it was, a shattered heart. My soul was working its way out in the cupped tears held in my eyes.

My grandma was *dea—*

My grandmother, of course, had been a part of me for as long as I could recall. She was always to be looked up to and respected, even when she painted her nails candy apple red and wore shiny gold sneakers, just to join us down the metal playground slide. Not only was she a vision of sass and undefined feminism, but she was also something so much more to me. In a world of familial angst, she buffered all of it with profound wisdom and wit greater than my universe.

I remember being a smallish child and feeling highly jealous of my cousin, Amber. She was tall and thin and beautiful to me. She was a gifted painter, sculptor, sketcher—you name it, she could do it all. It was evident that Amber was Grandma's favorite, and why wouldn't she be? It took many years and a motor vehicle accident later for me to realize that Grandma had just as much love for me too.

After my accident, Grandma and I began spending time together in the way that I had always dreamed of, and of course, by replacing Amber with myself. There were weekly movie dates and chain restaurant dinners that I never seemed to get enough of. As I went through college in a fiery storm of emotion, Grandma was the one there to greet me in my cheaply painted, white-walled apartment with neatly wrapped gifts on a Wednesday morning, if I needed her there. Although never much of a butcher, baker, nor candlestick maker, Grandma still tried her best and sent monthly brown paper wrapped packaged cookies and trinkets to keep my collegiate self satiated, with that undeniable sense of home that I was so blatantly lacking then.

Once I ironically found my way back to my hometown when adulthood finally kicked me out of college, Grandma and I began a weekly ritual of "America's Next Top Model." A guilty pleasure, contest show provided only on her cable television. I would arrive at her quaintly Southwestern decorated townhome that smelled mostly of old lipstick and crafting hot glue every single time.

The muted pastels and zigzagged edges spewed at every end of her home. The only reprise was a tall, glass shelf populated by hundreds of bells and angels. The bells, her own mother's obsession, while the angels were all Grandma's. She would cook reasonable chili, and I would clean my adobe-styled bowl every single time. We would chat about the latest model contestants and their lack of runway potential. We would both commiserate and giggle over nothing and everything. And our two unknowing, quite paralleled souls would play poker in the corner. Grandma was very easily one of the best friends I had ever had. Not only did I trust her every word, but I also trusted all the moments in between those words as well.

It wasn't long before Grandma began ordering pizza instead of concocting and burning stuff in the kitchen. I should have sensed it then, but shamefully part of me was relieved and ate the baked-in pepperoni in utter delight. Truthfully, I barely noticed anything until one Sunday afternoon.

Grandma had suggested this Asian restaurant. *Did she even know what sticky rice was?* Yet, I agreed without the slightest hesitation. I had been in a slump for quite some time, which was an equally colossal understatement. Wes had left for the Peace Corps a few months prior.

It was, however, during that lunch in which we were both attempting to take our minds off things, that Grandma was expressing my dad's love for–

"What's it? You know what it's called. It's that creamy stuff that you eat at breakfast?"

"Grandma, you mean oatmeal?"

"No, of course not oatmeeeeal. You know. Your dad just loves the stuff." She was starting to get a little uneasy about our verbal charades game, and so was I.

For several years now, I had noticed how Grandma had outgrown her own patience and began feeling exceptionally entitled to all of her feelings, no matter the cost. I chalked it up to getting older. I would imagine that the older you get and the longer you live, you probably no longer have room for the trivial junk. You begin to refuse that landfill anymore. Once you reach a certain age and junk-overflow, you receive some invisible badge that now allows you to tell that waitress that she could use to lose a few or your very own granddaughter that she is rude when she's late for lunch. I feel that I may take that badge rather reluctantly someday, but Grandma, Grandma took it like a champion on a podium of seniority.

"Cream of Wheat? Cream cheese? Yogurt?"

"Yes! Yogurt. Your dad loves yogurt." She exclaims in almost a "eureka!" like quality.

"Grandma, you're funny." *Why were we even talking about*

this again? Oh, right, as a simple distraction of my day. But what is it that Grandma needs a distraction from?

We finished up our sticky rice and green curry, both of which Grandma complained about relentlessly. We said our goodbyes, as Grandma was off to visit her daughter, Amber's mother and my Aunt Claire.

Claire, having been an oncology nurse my whole life, thought that Grandma's brief and cute memory lapses were neither brief nor cute and took her straight to the hospital. There was a looming shadow of a suspected stroke in the back of her mind, she later told us.

The darkened notion of a stroke, however, soon disappeared through a few CAT scans and MRI diagnostics. Grandma's films lit up like the embarrassingly competitive next-door neighbor during Christmas time.

It was cancer. It was in her brain. It was all over. Everywhere.

Somehow, I managed to keep myself quiet and stoic, possibly due to all the practice I had growing up. Not much was said from my dad regarding Grandma's state nor prognosis. I knew that he was devastated, but most people wouldn't even really tell. Although there was something in his tone and eyes that told me, not only that he was hurting, but also that he was human. The muscles in his face began to tense as well as ease up every time I saw him. He was raveling and unraveling at the same time.

I visited Grandma in the hospital with half of her head shaved, covered in an unnecessarily long and uncomforting bandage that reminded me of a grotesque turban. There were no tears, there was little reaction on my end, as I faced exactly none of it. She was strong and healthy, and she was going to recover, quickly.

Which she did exactly that.

See? I knew my grandma.

However, after several complaints of shoulder pain that echoed around anxious trick-or-treaters, Grandma found her way back to the oncologist recommended by Aunt Claire shortly before Thanksgiving. From there, gusty words like "hospice" and "terminal" came down and swooped in, stirring up everything my grandmother and our family had ever known. Those words took over and enveloped the sun. They ransacked the joint and left nothing unscathed, not even her heart.

By Christmas Eve, she could no longer walk, she would barely eat, and that ferocious and graceful spirit was left merely a flicker. We all gathered as we always did, this time at Claire's house, trying desperately to pretend everything was okay. She sat in silence for most of the night, observing her family and their gifts and conversations. She wore a vibrant red velour jumpsuit that I'm sure even she thought was pathetic. And I didn't even notice her shoes.

That Christmas changed everything. For the first time, I actually paid mind to my grandmother's deteriorating life. The rumors were, in fact, true.

She was dying.

With a heavy heart, I kept busy with coaching the high school girls' swim team and Wes' sudden and unexpected return from the Peace Corps.

Wes had returned a whole year early in a grand gesture to follow his heart. *Wouldn't it have been so perfect if he had returned for me? To be with me during this time of great suffering and need*? Too bad his heart was trailing a mousey Asian accountant from LA.

I had been avoiding visiting my grandmother. My throat burned to admit it. She had moved into her brother's home as a final destination retreat, which scared me more than that musky hospice facility she had come from. She had given away all of her worldly possessions, spreading them out like the ashes of a life that couldn't exist anymore.

Finally, I sucked in that stinging breath and agreed to meet my dad over at the house to visit with Grandma. It was a brilliantly sun-shiny January morning. I could even hear faint sounds of birds commenting on the glorious day. My dad hung up the phone after planning to help me up the front stairs and then hopefully stay the hell away from me. I didn't have the slightest idea of how to behave as a grieving granddaughter in front of all these familial strangers. And, I certainly didn't have the energy to figure it out beforehand. I can just wing it, and shimmy myself out the door if it becomes too much. *What is too much?*

We arrived at virtually the same time. Although, truth be told, I had been circling the house for nearly a half hour. My dad barely said a word other than joking about it being difficult lifting my chair up the stairs. I smiled a soft, courteous smile and pushed myself over the door jamb into the foyer of the house. Grandma was staying in the extra bedroom, but it appeared to look more like a makeshift hospital room than anything. Monitors were beeping and my disintegrating grandmother lay somewhere in the middle of the plug-in bed.

I found my way to her side immediately. There was little left in her eyes, and less in her body.

I never knew you could watch somebody die before.

She tried to speak.

"Ooooohh, you want the TV on?" Aunt Claire insisted as my dad picked up the remote control and began firing away. He was a master marksman of the remote and could probably seek much solace in changing those channels. However, it was clear to me that was not what Grandma was trying to say at all.

She raised her hand nearest mine, and I grabbed it as if I had been waiting my whole life for that moment. She uttered and sputtered again, to little reprieve. Her jaw crackled as she tried to speak. My dad was still clicking through the weekend news and sports reports while Aunt Claire was working as the professional nurse and caregiver that she was. Her calm and sensitive demeanor made the updates on oxygen stats and heart numbers sound like a poem.

But Grandma was trying to say something, and she was trying to say it to me. *Didn't anyone else understand this?*

Within minutes, I was whisked away by both Aunt Claire and Dad, who said that Grandma needed her rest and that I could return tomorrow if I wanted. I promised Grandma, with a delicate squeeze to her tiny hand, that I would be back tomorrow, smiled the most forced smile I have ever performed, and wheeled out of the room.

I managed to hold a world's worth of tears in my eyelids until I got in my car. Alone, I cried for hours. Alone, I wished for so many moments–both past and future–for me and Grandma to share.

I felt *true* desperation for losing someone I love.

I should have known my promise to Grandma would be broken. Known that would be the last time that I would ever see her again. I felt it. I felt it in her squeeze and saw it in her nearly extinguished eyes.

I have never been a breaker of promises, so I neglected any preparation for my visit and headed over the following afternoon. The sun didn't appear to penetrate my windshield the way it did the day before, and I couldn't make out any tweeting or chortling or anything brilliant about my day.

Dad and I had planned for much of the same, yet this time Abby was supposed to meet us as well. I was only three turns away when I received a call from my dad. All that he said was, "Hurry."

But I knew I was too late. I knew I was too late before the phone even rang. Something about the world out of my windshield seemed so different, so foreign. The birds had tried to warn me, I suppose, by not playing their beautiful songs for me. Suddenly, the world became so blaring yet muddled. The sun was making me itchy and blinded. All sounds became slowed and muffled. *I guess I keep going.*

Just as the day before, Dad greeted me, but this time, without a word. He shuffled me up the four stairs into the dark entryway like a delivery man who hates his job.

Everyone was there.

No one spoke.

I was too late.

I couldn't face anyone, let alone myself. With all the strength that I had remaining in my body, I asked my dad to let me down the stairs. "I have to leave." Each word stung and ached. Every breath felt constricted and unfulfilled. He obliged and asked if I was okay. *Of course, I'm not okay. Are you insane? Do you even have the smallest idea of what has happened here? To her? To me?* I nodded.

For a moment, sitting in my car, alone once again, I thought I might just die too.

Somehow, I managed to drive straight home, but barely made it past the front door. Less than a couple of feet inside, I pulled myself out of my wheelchair and onto the scratchy carpeted floor in a puddle of tears and sorrow. I covered myself with the first thing I could grab, my camping sleeping bag. I couldn't breathe under that bag, but I also didn't want to. It smelled of campfire and dirt, and now the sorrow and tears for Grandma. My face hurt so badly, as it laid sopping wet and pressed into the commercial-grade apartment carpet. I switched sides as I traded one sore side of my face to allow it to rest.

My tears were everywhere, and they were endless. I wished for my Grandma. I wished for another minute with her. I wished she could tell me what to do next.

There were hours where I wasn't sure if I'd ever have the strength to get back into my chair, and there were hours where I wasn't sure if I'd ever want to. My tear-soaked face felt raw from that scratchy carpet, and my breath was becoming campfirey and labored too. I probably needed to pee, but I couldn't find the strength nor care to do anything about any of it. The rest of the day and into the dark of night I lied there. I found myself whispering, "Goodnight Grandma" as I finally fell asleep that night. It may have been hours, and it may have been days.

Goodnight Grandma.

the blip

WHEN ALL SEEMS LOST, sometimes it's best to get lost too for a while. That feeling of loss and being lost takes all of your control away—leaving you vulnerable and scared. If you don't do something about it, it will continue to take all of you. I couldn't let that happen.

I purchased a foreclosed property up in the foothills the day after my grandma died. It needed so much work. Apparently, I did too.

Rebuilding and recreating something from less-than-functional or dilapidated resources has always been a forte of mine, at least as long as I can remember. Having been forced into a less-than-functional body at a young age, I was always forced to improvise to the best of my abilities. And, to be truthful, I didn't mind the daily challenge so much. Being challenged in that way—even just putting my own pants on—was building me up and making me stronger and more cognizant each day. That was, each day that I allowed myself to confront it. So, it was no surprise when I stumbled upon that early 1940s home in the shallow hills, off any beaten path I had ever known, and fell in love with it immediately.

Being in my early twenties, I couldn't imagine anything better than owning my own home. This home was raw yet historic. It appeared overlooked and in need of love and held my heart immediately. The siding was a difficult shade of brown, high-lighted with the most uncomfortable shade of olive-green vomit bleeding through. As you approached the front stoop, there were numerous broken glass windowpanes, surrounded by the most beautiful frozen garden of best intentions. It was all danger and fear, surrounded by the hope for growth.

Inside, the walls were bare at best. Some walls had obvious mold, while others had been painted with images of SpongeBob SquarePants and broken mirror shards placed every so strategically to look like the smiling sun. How could I not love this place?

The hardwood floors creaked and cracked as I rolled through, traversing room to room—falling deeper and deeper in love with the place. The only bedroom donned a mossy, sponge-colored green carpet and faux wood paneling. Broken fixtures intermixed with the dirt and dinge that let me know that this place was once loved by others too. Broken beer bottles and underwear suggested that perhaps there were others that made this home their own, most likely without the proper paperwork.

Somewhere inside of me, I knew Grandma would want nothing more for me than to have it. So, on the very day of Grandma's funeral services, I found my way to a small juice café wearing black knee-high boots and swollen eye sockets. I met my realtor with a desperate smile and limp handshake.

Sign on the dotted line. I whispered over and over again, trying desperately to summon the strength from my grandmother as I inhaled between those soft chants.

In fact, I still think of it as Grandma's house today.

The timing was everything. I had been looking for a way to be an adult for months. Words like "*investment*" and "*savings*" had just become a recent addition to my, rather, juvenile vocabulary. I was best when talking with teenagers—what their swim strokes look like and how to pass English class. However, those conversations were so often one-dimensional, so they were typically balanced out with proper scaffolding by Grandma and even Faye. But Grandma hadn't spoken for months, and I'm not sure how much Faye wanted to talk about finances. Gandhi—yes, mortgages—not yet.

My "investment" vision quickly transformed from desiring a small plot of land in which I could sustainably and foolishly build a freestanding yurt upon, to rashly purchasing a fairly aged and warn would-be home from long ago. It was clear that it had been some time since this home had been loved. And I loved that.

Probably the most appealing part of this house was that it had to be fixed. There was no way someone could purchase it and move into the mess and heaps of garbage and broken glass. Someone had to care enough, have enough guts, and a slightness for insanity to make this thing theirs. That person was definitely me.

An implied scent of rotting pipes and feral water emanated from every pore of every barely insulated wall. Each time I visited, I wanted to hold my breath for the stench, but I couldn't because I was always required to convince appraisers and contractors exactly why I loved this house.

The strange thing is that I did love it, at first sight, and smell even. It was something about the combination of floor-to-ceiling windows and outdated lanterns that hung low and even from each window. The windows led to an untouched world of soft green leaves that varied from everything needled and brilliant to secrets of the broad and muted. They were exactly what I would imagine windows to my home to be. I would suppose I chose the real-life version of the windows to my soul.

Signing for those rights and that adulthood the exact same day of my grandmother's funeral, I knew right at that moment that those windows were going to be important for my healing. They were going to be important for my growth too, as my eyes took in the giant blue spruce and soldier-like aspen tree stands that offered me all my comfort.

The house was now mine. A single, mid-twenties wheel-chair woman with not even a single cat to explain the absurdity, now with her very own stale-underwear scented den. Breathing in Grandma's strength was going to be the only way to keep moving.

I had lived on my own in apartments for so many years leading up, but for some reason, changing the title to "homeowner" made a significant difference in my accessibility and persistence to be independent. In all reality, my so-called independence is nothing more than a self-glorified stubbornness coupled with a dusting of misunderstood optimism.

Being the new owner of a "new" very old house, I couldn't help but relate it to the feeling of sudden, yet foreshadowing, rainfall amid radiant sunshine. There were so many things to consider that had never been on my radar before, not even a blip.

Blip. That word is so interesting.

Historically speaking, that word came into play in the late 1800s and was meant to describe a punch or tap, to a sprinkling of authors at the time. It was more akin to a sound. But somehow, someone somewhere decided to change it entirely to its more or less scientific meaning we use today. Unexpected change of something.

Blip.

If it were up to me, I'd prefer the original notion—it seems far more fitting. The word alone even sounds like its description. And, what a history, to be able to just change the meaning of a word through a few dozen years? I suppose that if a sudden and startling deviation of a thing needed a sound to match, *blip* would be it. It all makes so much sense to me now. All of it.

"These colors are not colors that ... uh, that people ... uh, *use.*" There was an exaggeration to that word "use" that I didn't quite care to recognize. My contractor was stern and stoic like my father, and his droopy mustache helped him also appear eternally sad.

"What do you mean? You told me to pick out colors for my walls, so I did." I wasn't going to be afraid of him. It wasn't like he was going to yell or send me to my room or anything, right?

"People just don't paint their walls orange, or limy green, or that strange pink color ..."

"It's called Fiesta Fuchsia."

"Well, don't you want to look at some books or something to make sure? I'm bettin' you can find some real nice colors in design books or if you ask the folks at the hardware store down the street."

"I did ask them, and they told me to choose colors that I was drawn to, colors that I wouldn't get tired of, and colors that would make me happy."

"Make you happy?" "Okay, I added that part."

"Whatever. Fine." And that was that. Although my contractor and I saw little in common, especially regarding the well-being of my mental status in conjunction with my understanding of the color wheel, he did his part to make sure that this house was going to work for me. And, although he didn't speak much or smile ever, he did always offer ideas of how to make my house more accessible for me. In the end, I know he did it because he was kind and caring, but that stale, saggy mustache was really not helping him out one bit.

I took in his considerations and held them to my heart to get a good feel for them. He could lower countertops, raise sinks, secure grab bars, and remove stairs. He was an accessibility miracle worker with a hammer in his belt, yet I wasn't about to take advantage of any of it.

I prefer to call it *stubborn*. I fear most would just call it *stupid*.

I had never fully lived in a place that was totally accessible for a wheelchair, and I wasn't about to start. I didn't know how to live like that, but I did know very much about using hangers to get cups down from an overhead cabinet and sitting in the bathtub to take spritzing far-away showers. Although, come to think of it, I really do dread turning on that bone-chilling shower water early in the morning. I never have the chance to fully miss its startling spray from where I sit. *But it's fine.*

My stubbornness and unwillingness to show any attention to my wheelchair may be both my greatest asset as well as my most tragic flaw. I always wanted people to just see me and pay no mind to the fact that I may be different, or even focus on abilities that people clearly take for granted. It's so hard. My wheelchair has so much to do with it all as much as it doesn't. *Poor guy, you stood no fighting chance against this unyielding and convoluted psyche.*

With a furrowed brow to match his mustache, and a sense of defeat, that silly contractor man was sent on his way with little to do other than build a wooden ramp in the entrance of this new dilapidated kingdom. I purchased it on my very own—with the strength of Grandma standing by—and wasn't going to let that zest run out any time soon.

I was now responsible for things like hot water heaters and ventilation systems, which I clearly knew nothing about. That radar of mine was now lighting up with storms of electrical conundrums and appliance failures. A stop or two at the local hardware store in town became part of my routine. This soon proved to be more volatile than any turpentine whiff, when Wes walked back into my life.

He had since returned home from Paraguay after a failed attempt at pursuing something that wasn't actually his dream.

He thought it was, but somehow, he had lied to himself too.

Only a couple months after I left him to his *guampa* and his hut building in the remoteness of South American farmland, Wes stumbled upon something that I pretended not to witness for myself. He had fallen in love with someone that wasn't me.

I looked back at our last few months together, apart. I should have seen it coming.

"Hi, I'm just trying to get in touch with you again. You seem to be really busy ... I guess that's good. Call me?" I began communicating with this voicemail more frequently than anything else. *Was I losing him? Did I actually ever have him?*

Those months wore on me and broke down virtually everything we had created, and even though I knew it and felt it in his every word, I held on. I suppose I held on for nostalgia's sake and for a lack of knowing where or how to breathe alone. Neither of those things were enough to combat the distance and his, quite literal, wanderlust heart.

Wes quit the Peace Corps after only half of his commitment, partially disenchanted by the stubborn townspeople in the village who didn't want his help in the first place. And conversely, he was more-than-partially *en*chanted by another half-committed volunteer stationed in the same lonely town in Paraguay.

In a whirlwind of email exchanges, confusing SMS messages at all hours of the night, and not being able to connect at the right time on the phone, our relationship was over. I felt my world was too.

If it wasn't for that house that I had believed in from the start, I could have ended up in a much darker spot altogether. That house though, it really needed me.

Wes' transformation was deep rooted. It was far bigger than his sway of heart. I often still wonder if he experienced a genuine change in his character, or if his true character had just been revealed for the first time.

He no longer respected his minimalistic view of the things—rather he thought it foolhardy. He wanted to make the most money that he could in the easiest and fastest manner he could muster. Lucky for him, he was a well-witted, borderline genius, when he wanted to be. Band because of it, had set his sights on the most applicable way he could financially advance himself in the world: by becoming an anesthesiologist.

He returned home with his newly beating heart, and we tried to remain surface friends. You know, friends that don't dig any deeper than exactly what is in front of them on the surface? That was going to be the only way to expect him in my life.

Please don't show me your roots. Bury them deep.

He made his new life plans and tried sharing them with me, although I was still uncertain if I wanted to listen. To get back on his feet, he started working at the hardware store in town. In *my* new town. Near *my* new house.

How fitting.

He, single-handedly, had stepped into and onto my new world of growth. SPLAT! And although he most likely didn't intentionally try to squash it, he sure did his damnedest to show up in the paint sample aisle or plumbing fixtures section every single time.

"How's the house coming?" He pressed each word, so nonchalantly I thought each one would kill me.

"Fine. Great. I'm happy! I love it!" I hated these interactions because they took so much away from the fact that I *was* actually happy about my new home and its renovations. I wished he wouldn't feel the need to connect, it would make everything so much easier. *How could he make both my stomach crawl and heart ache at the same time?*

I left the store without remembering anything I walked in for. I was so frazzled about his impact on my new happiness. It wasn't fair. This house was a way for me to move on, yet he was making it dangerously difficult for me to see any growth.

It was finally more than I could take. I couldn't justify driving another twenty miles down the mountain to try out a different, ex-boyfriendless hardware store. Nor could I manage pretending to be okay. It was so painful to swallow so much lingering emotion.

Driving straight back to my house, I brushed off the dust piling at the only table I had, and began working on the only thing I could. I needed to write him a letter.

I wrote, and wrote, and wrote. I tore out pages and started again. I smudged words with my tears, and then wrote all over again. And, then just like that, I popped it in the mail, addressed to his mother's house, making the assumption that he wasn't too far back on his feet to have his own place yet.

I squeezed the envelope tightly, but not too much to wrinkle it. But I didn't want him to know I had thought so much to give it such care, so I squeezed it anyway. And then it was clear. It was blaring and pulsing in my grey matter: He was my blip.

Then in the most demonstrative and cathartic way, I held the envelope over the darkened mail slot and with a deep breath in, I let go ...

conducting the great whites

"YOU KNOW, YOU SHOULD REALLY become a teacher." The voice was strong and intentional, some sort of voice that I had always longed to emulate myself. It was also familiar, familiar yet strange enough to rip me out of my reverie at that moment. The face behind the voice was a recognizable one indeed. Blinking twice, I was brought back to the real world.

I had been coaching ever since I was discharged from the hospital after my accident. I think as sort of a we-are-not-really-sure-what-to-do-with-you-now job offer. The team hired me on as a junior coach, but I was quick to prove to them that I was going to swim for them as well. I knew no other way.

Coaching, and those squawky team mothers who decided that fate for me, created a turning point for me that I wouldn't quite realize until many years later. It was a well-intended, yet pathetic, moment creating the swim coach position for me. I can only imagine the conversations behind that. Yet, I will forever be grateful for those swim moms who didn't know how else to coddle me and made me their kids' coach.

I was coaching the high school team that I had graduated from not too long ago. And there I was, overdressed, sitting in the middle of a banquet hall in a suburban hotel, listening to my swim team teenagers attempt their best at the podium. They were pubescent-poised and thanking their families and guffawing about the friends they had made throughout the season.

The year-end swim team hoopla was in full swing. There were blue and red suited teddy bears for centerpieces on each table. Sparkly blue and red cardboard cutouts hung high from the ceilings. Awards were given, and tears flowed, only to wait for when we could do it all again next year. I felt so much more comfortable in this setting as a coach, rather than a swimmer. I found so much comfort in helping others. It was far easier than helping myself.

I was proud of those girls, and the accomplishments that they had made during the season. But it wasn't those blue-ribbon champions that made me most proud—it was being able to be a tour guide along for the ride of each of their adolescent lives. It mattered little to me if they won or lost, and much more to me the process that they took to get there. I watched each girl, dressed in her best, dry hair and all, and hoped that I taught them something. I wished I had taught them the things I had learned, just easier or sooner. I wanted to be a catalytic coach for kids in those years that are the cruelest and most often fraught.

Dr. Jones was one of the most poised women I had ever met. She had hired me and brought me back to this pride for the team. She had been *my* catalyst in taking me away from my own insecurities and doubts. *Oh, thank you!*

She was, and had been, the principal at the high school since the dawn of the Ice Age, I suspected. Not for age, but rather for the roots she had laid in the community. She had a softened face with a stern tongue. I admired her for being able to embody both. I admired her for being a woman in charge. When she spoke, everyone would listen, for those were the only words that would ever be heard at such a moment. Such a moment like this one.

"A teacher? Pardon? Me?" I whispered, adding a dramatic pause in every place that I could. I tried hard not to cause my voice to quiver or sound as weak as it felt approaching my pharynx.

"We should talk. You are a natural." It was all that she said to me, as the applause of the crowds of young teen girls around me whisked her onto the stage to give her yearly speech of accomplishment and desire to push to one's own limit. I was left to my thoughts.

As Dr. Jones spoke, she spoke of putting yourself, full-bodied, into the task at hand. She spoke of guts and the honor that one achieves when you really go for it. At that moment, she was speaking only to me. Clearly, she wasn't. But it didn't matter. I chose that moment for myself and myself only. The applause returned as she said goodnight to the crowd. That applause, raucous yet polite, surrounded me and felt as if it were made for me too.

I looked around at the clapping crowd. The girls, all with their parents, all standing for Dr. Jones and her powerful words. Each of those girls held smiles of a million joyful opportunities.

I couldn't get it out of my mind as I left the hotel and headed home. As the days passed, I found myself searching harder and harder for the "Top 10 Reasons I Hate My Job," and came up with double that. I had been working as a dressed-up legal assistant by pure happenstance, yet little joy. I had a job that many wanted, and would fight me for. They can all have it. The business attire and paper piles. The office gossip and keyboard clacking. It was not for me, and never was for me no matter how hard I clacked and gossiped in return.

It wasn't long before I got up the nerve. That nerve, though, came from deep within. I had to reach far down into my spirit, sifting through whimsy and rainbowed matter. I had to push those things aside for the tiny, powdered bits of courage made just for this moment.

I picked up the phone. It was as if she had known I was going to call at that very moment. Dr. Jones knew just about everything, about everything.

There was no nervous interview, no sweaty-palmed handshakes, or even ridiculous triple-intentional questions about my "free time" or "hobbies." I didn't have to even iron out my insufferable business attire. Dr. Jones had already spoken with the head of the science department about me, and I was good—as good as gastropods in the rain!

I was going to be a teacher.

It was set, and they had laid out the plan before me, long before I could even think about any repercussions or anxieties. As I have found, in all of my life, that the best and most poignant decisions have always been made with little effort on my part. I have felt many moments of skating through clouds and unicorn dust brushing against my cheeks as paths have been chosen for me. In a blink, jobs, relationships, and so much in between have been initiated all while I practice my perfected and sparkly triple Lutz, with little regard to actual decision-making of the thing.

I have always been a hopeless fatalist and have had so much practice at just letting go with the wind of the universe. So much so that I not only have learned to trust it, but I have also learned to expect it. I expect the universe to hold my hand and lead me to where I am supposed to be.

It is with those very feelings that I have come to understand so much more about life. Those things in life that you are intended to experience will, indeed, happen. Those things will take their course. You will learn, and grow, no matter what space you occupy, no matter how oblivious you are, even no matter how much you may try to avoid it. Forward motion is inevitable. You may as well be smiling along for that ride, with the trust that everything will turn out okay in the end. The power of the universe is not something I would like to match up against. TKO me, the universe will always win.

Everyone has a path to take, and everyone has specific stops along their self-determined, yet chosen, paths. Those stops are simply part of the journey of what makes you, you. All paths lead to OZ, no matter which direction you choose. The cowardly lion may skip with you, or he may not. That part is for you to decide.

Luckily for me, I decided early on to trust what the universe had offered up to me in shooting stars and accidental smiles. If I hadn't been able to relinquish some of my own control to the unsettling unknown, I may have never learned how to fall on that ice. It's almost more important to know how to fall than to actually perform that triple Lutz you've been practicing.

After all, how would I have ever gone on with living if I didn't trust everything would be alright in the end? I needed to look beyond paralysis, alcoholism, and unintentional teenage isolation to something better on the horizon. That is what we called coping, at its very finest. It was my "Survival of the Fittest," and in order for me to survive, I had to learn how to deal with the world. It's as simple as that. I had to choose not to harbor ill feelings for the world or let myself believe that it wasn't fair. I had to, with all parts of my being, decide that I was going to live because everything was going to work out the way it was intended to.

People are so quick to rush their path that they may race right by something that was better suited for them in the end. People can be so pushy, especially with themselves and, better yet, the idea of themselves. But not me. I was happy to hold the hand of destiny and follow it wherever it might take me. No, no, you go first.

And so, without question, I took that hand, and a job as a full-time physical science teacher intending to enrich the minds of the youngest high school souls. These wide eyes were still merely eighth graders with chips on little shoulders carrying less-than-little backpacks. But, to me, they were Great White Sharks circling my boat above. Were they going to think I was too young? Were they going to eat me alive? See, Great White Sharks are not only brawn. They are known for their beefy exterior and absurdly frightening smile, yet they have proved to be highly intelligent predators as well. My students were the same.

I had less than a month to prepare for this new path. Seemingly appearing out of nowhere for me, I was now driving down this road, going at it one hundred miles per hour. Yet, there weren't enough dry erase markers in the world that were going to fully prime me for this gig.

Entering a world of teenage pranksters and flailing hormones, there was little I could do but follow those around me. They assigned me to a mentor teacher, who had chosen the noble role of teaching the new teachers all the tricks that they had found in their mastered state of academia. My mentor was Tiffany, a bubbly, well-dressed early thirty-something-year-old with a yearning to be admired. There was no doubt that she wanted to be admired by her students, admired by her friends, admired by her boyfriend (of which she enunciated at every chance she could get), and now admired by me.

After only a few brief meetings in my office between class sessions, I quickly understood that Tiffany was a woman who loved to talk. Unfortunately, she loved to talk mostly about herself.

In those few short weeks, I learned so much about her family, her apartment, her annoying neighbor, and of course, "the boyfriend." As she talked, she flipped her caramel dyed hair, and as she talked, my mind would wander ... *Shouldn't I be learning about classroom management or lesson planning or something? Why does she think she needs that perfume? Does she stink underneath it?* But, alas, I think her cat spilled her coffee on her new imported Persian rug or something. I nodded to her with a furrowed brow, hopefully telling her that I completely understood the situation and story of the moment.

Weeks of this went by, when finally, we had a breakthrough.

Tiffany suggested that in order to gain better control over my little post-tweeny rug rats, I was to turn the lights off when I wanted them to be quiet. I would plan a session in advance to practice that skill with them prior to utilizing it to better prepare them for the enforcement. I surrendered to her seniority on the matter with a big sigh, although I was picturing those Great Whites laughing at me.

This just so happened to be a lesson in which my direct supervisor, the head of the science department, Mr. Langley, was to observe my class session. Mr. Langley seemed to hide softly behind his large-lens glasses. He wasn't a man of stature in height, but he certainly was in presence. His hiding eyes were kind, rivaling his ever-present, unintentional smile. His features softened him outwardly, but internally he was wound like a clock. The man couldn't sit still.

And, although I absolutely adored and admired Mr. Langley, I was also incredibly terrified of his potential impressions of me. I so wanted him to like me, but even more, I wanted him to think of me as a good teacher. He sat in the back of the classroom, virtually unnoticed by the youngsters surrounding him. This was exactly how he intended it to be, as he heavily scribbled the things I could only imagine on his rolled-up yellow legal pad.

"Now, when I do this ..." I articulated in a long and drawn-out manner, in order to match my very own long and drawn-out extravagant motion to the light switch, "you will stop talking.

Let's try. Now talk a bunch." I motioned like a conductor to my symphony.

The kids just stared at me. I stared back and then subtly switched my gaze to Mr. Langley who was writing furiously, while keeping his eyes, cocked and questioning, on my chosen conducting.

Mr. Langley was truly, in every sense, a master teacher. He loved science, he loved his students, and he loved teaching his students science. That made him great. However, he was also a tornado of a human being, with papers and varied yellow notepads piled beyond his less-than-stealthy five-foot-tall frame. His office was held together by piles of textbooks and notebooks, as well as pictures that students had drawn for him. That made him great too.

Curiously, he seemed to always walk at an angle with his forehead positioned slightly forward the rest of his body. It was as if he never had enough time to actually get to wherever he was going. It was either that or, I suspected, that his body couldn't keep pace with his brilliant brain. He was someone that I deeply admired. He was an educator of perpetual motion.

As the class bell rang, metaphorically saving me from much more of a disaster, my hungry Great Whites scurried and swam away to their next potential bait. Mr. Langley walked straight up to the front of the classroom, weaving between giant backpacks and tiny lab desks. Typically, Mr. Langley would just leave out the backdoor as soon as the bell emitted any sort of frequency at all. He seemed to appear and disappear like magic most days. But, not today. He moved toward me at full-angle.

"Why did you do that?" He huffed. He was blunt and to the point, exactly everything that I wish he wasn't at that moment. *Hadn't he ever heard of a "compliment sandwich"?*

First off, give me a high five or a pat on the back for pronouncing that one new kid's name right, or even compliment me on the fact that I wore a skirt today. Give me something. Didn't he ever learn the "compliment sandwich" technique in *his* teacher school? Tiffany gushed about that on the first day, conveniently just after an unappetizing bit of boyfriend woes and how-do-you-dos.

"Uh, I ... I ... I guess Tiffany suggested it as a way for me to manage my class better. I suppose I could try it again tomorrow ..." *Stop it! You are rambling!* "Or perhaps, I could try something a little different. Perhaps I could ring a bell. Yes! She suggested that too ..." *Oh, please stop! For your own sake, for your own good. Close your mouth!* "Or even ..."

"Now, this is making sense." He paused in an extremely comfortably uncomfortable sort of way. The pause made me guess his next move. Never guess Mr. Langley's next move. "Tiffany suggested this?" He remarked as calmly as I had ever seen this little man utter. He didn't move, other than his finger shaking in the air as his clock began winding up again.

"Yes?"

"I think that may have been the problem. See, that isn't you. You don't need her advice to manage your classroom. Look no further than your own gut. You'll be able to relate and run your classroom so much better, and with better ease, if you just follow what you already know to be true. You hold your authority and the students' attention, even from a sitting position. That's an extremely difficult thing to do." I hadn't thought of that, in this classroom or the entire world that I sat in. But he was right.

He waved his hand behind him as he scurried out my classroom door, now unseen amongst similar-height teenagers moving every which way down the hall. Students weaved in and out of time and space, and my world managed to get quiet and still for a minute.

I breathed in the words of Mr. Langley and let them stir in my mind. Students arriving for the next class piled in, jumping and dancing about as they made their way to their assigned seats. I gave some of them soft waves, some hellos, and even a high five. They didn't notice my new smile.

The bell rang, and brought me back to life. The ring sounded so sweet and optimistic. Taking another big breath in, I made sure to breathe in that moment with Mr. Langley one more time.

Flipping my wheelchair around to conduct all over again, I announced, "Good afternoon, young Great Whites!"

the *me* staring back at me

IT DIDN'T EVEN LOOK LIKE ME. I tried squinting. I tried smiling and swaying. I knew that those blued, wide-set eyes were familiar, and the scars were unmistakable, but what was staring back at me was hardly recognizable.

Those leg braces. Those scrap metal inklings of human scaffolding traced the exact outlines of both my atrophied legs. Worn leather and leftover Velcro straps hugged each section of each leg, just how you'd expect awkward ex-lovers may embrace during an accidental reunion. My legs were forced straight and stretched all the way from the platform of the parallel bars upward to the point where legs turn into torso. I was standing ... or so I was told that's what it was to be called.

With white knuckles and quivering biceps, I attempted to allow my brain to think of this event as standing too. Since that's what everyone else was calling it. You know, I'm jumping off the bridge too.

Those crude braces, that were clearly doing all the work, had been the manual labor of a youngish Indian prosthetic maker, inappropriately named Akroor. Inappropriate only because his name meant "kind," that of which he ever proved to be anything but. Akroor, although far less knowledgeable in the English language than at brace-making, took much effort in translating to me his utter disgust for both my contracted hips and restricted legs, as well as the person who agreed to house such a mess of a body. Perhaps it was a real blessing that Akroor and I never had the chance at a meaningful conversation about anything. I had a feeling he would have simply rolled his nearly blackish eyes and explained to me that I was disgusting.

Lucky for me, my encounters with Akroor were few. He only visited the clinic when there was a problem with my make-shift leg braces, which, one can suspect, was rare given a mere two-month period of trial.

I had only been in India for less than a week's time, and on one hand it felt like a lifetime, but on the other less than a reactive flinch of time. Smells of garam masala and burning trash filled the air, and my limbic system was busy creating those memories out of the unusual scents.

From that point onward, I would always think of India when I smelled things burning. Don't get me wrong though, India was amazing. I was settled in the hustle of New Delhi, and I couldn't feel more at home, although lacking the connection of language with most I encountered. Quick enough, I learned you could easily get by with a simple head bob and a smile.

I had made this journey with Faye, Eve—and another one of my dearest friends and travel companions—Margot, in my back pocket. I had ripped each of them straight out of the early twenty-something journey that they had separately been living. They were each there only because of me. I knew that.

Squinting, I tried desperately to keep them and their glowing smiles out of my view while staring back at myself. I wasn't going to allow myself to take for granted the sacrifices that each of these girls were making for me, to be my support system, so far from home.

Dr. Mehra was walking toward me, and I knew, not because I could see her in the mirrored reflection, but because her essence was just that powerful. She was an extremely petite woman who spoke very precise, well-thought-out statements only in necessary encounters. Not only was she conscientious with her intentions, but she was also extremely conscientious with her intimidations. I was scared to death of her on most levels, but, at the same moment, very much wanted to give her a large double-armed bear hug and have her say nice things about me.

"Looks like you are walking much better today than yesterday," was all that was said from her proportionately petite mouth. "The stem cells are, no doubt, starting to find their way ..." I had noticed she dropped a lot of her sentences in a strategic, yet subtle manner. I have determined that it was, in part, due to the dramatic nature of dropping phrases like losing your breath. But also because nobody knew a thing about the nature of these extremely blank, yet potent and controversial cells that they had now been injecting in my body for a little over a week.

Dr. Mehra had been performing stem cell treatments for a few years at that time, becoming increasingly more and more paranoid by the moment. She was smart enough to know that she had stumbled upon a goldmine. She was also smart enough to know that she had no clue what was going to be the most effective way of extracting this metaphorical *gold*. So she kept skeptically quiet about it all.

Her controversial work first came to my attention when I found out that a woman who became a teenage mentor to me so many years ago, a perfect sample of paraplegic beauty, had found her way to stem cell treatments in India and found her way back into my life.

I first recognized Angela on the news. I was in immediate shock. This woman was so perfect in my eyes, and had always been. Yet, she was unhappy with her own prognosis? She didn't find it alright to settle in her wheelchair? It practically exploded my mind to find out that this figure of wheeled confidence, my very first mentor, wanted so badly to rid herself of her wheelchair that she would even fly across continents to attempt it. So, I did the only thing I thought I could think of. I telephoned Angela and asked to meet her again.

When we met, she startled me with her beauty and confidence all over again. She spoke in such a soothing manner that she probably could have convinced me of virtually anything. Yet, as she spoke, I gathered her sights were set slightly higher than mine. Angela wanted to walk again. Angela was going to fly around the world as many times as it took to do it. Her beauty resonated with me immediately, and she spoke as if everything was a sonnet. I was all ears.

In our brief meeting, she showed me all of her new tricks. How she could pick up one leg that was dangling off her wheelchair's footrest and replace it, ever so gently using reawakened muscles. She told me how she could feel things that she hadn't in decades. She was talking miracles, and I was holding on to every word. By the time we hugged goodbye, I had made my decision.

I wanted to go to India too.

My decision came from silent whispers in my soul that refused to entertain my desire to walk, but rather contemplated something much more graspable—my overall longevity.

Being a paraplegic with a spinal cord injury definitely had its perks. Like getting pushed into the front of lines at amusement parks and dance clubs, convenient parking wherever you go, and never having the need to find a seat in a crowded café. However, that is precisely where those benefits ended.

Having lost the natural ability to walk, left me with a poor-to-nonexistent circulatory system, a proneness to wounds that would not heal, as well as an incessant strain on my heart and other vital organs. This was all because man had not endured evolution for millions of years just to sit in a chair all day long.

Few that I told understood beyond a desire to walk again. They heard what they wanted to. Walking, to most, appeared to be the only thing that separated me from the rest of the world. And isn't that everyone's ultimate goal—to be like everyone else? Outwardly, my wheels made me different, but there was so much more that my insides couldn't actually express outwardly. That made me different too.

I had already spent over a decade with these wheels inter-meshed in my personal identity. If I were walking, where would that identity go? *Would it find a new rabbit hole to jump into? Would it be engulfed into the night air? Would it, lonely and disgruntled, seek revenge by sabotaging my new frolicking, foot-stepping identity?* I had so many questions for myself.

Finally, acknowledging the demons of my body and its inces-sant questioning, I made the decision. I was to follow Angela in those very few first footsteps and travel to New Delhi, India, to receive an almost unheard-of stem cell treatment. It was far less about the journey toward walking than it was about being around long enough to teach the someday-kids of my own to take their own first steps. To be honest, I may never be fully certain of the exact one thing that drove me to take that leap. Sometimes those things are better left in the shadows.

And now, there I was in sweet and salty smelling India, propped up, standing up, and sweating skeptically to the *me* staring back at me.

I was feeling somewhat different—stronger, more balanced, more complete—but was I crazy? I quickly swallowed any excitement elicited by these thoughts and went back to focusing on my immediate concerns with the mirror, again focusing not to catch eyes with any of my onlookers.

At that very moment, the world stopped in its place to give me a much-needed moment to think. This is something I didn't allow myself to do often enough in my everyday life.

Like magic, the world froze around me.

Babies were silenced in mid-cry.

A man relieved himself on the not-so-private back wall of the clinic emitted a paused yellow stream and a rather proud pose.

Grass stopped growing, and old ladies stopped shrinking.

Everything was still. Everything had frozen in time, just for me. This was my moment, so I had to make it good.

Along with the babies, and pee-ers, and grasses, and old ladies, everyone in the clinic was frozen too. Everything was stopped, allowing me to regain myself and recollect my deepest wisdoms. *What the hell was I doing here?*

Once I had officially decided to follow this path to New Delhi, it became immediately evident the amount of power that my paralysis paralyzed everyone else. I had no idea how much my inability to walk affected everyone else around me. I had even less of an idea of how tragic others viewed my life. Even to those closest to me.

Finalizing my decision—fundraising, buying plane tickets, talking to Indian doctors at odd hours—I became more and more bombarded by the "hope" of walking again. *But wait just one minute!* That wasn't *my* dream. That wasn't *my* goal, but now I felt somewhat compelled to go along with the crowd. That cheering and hooting crowd displaying ear-to-ear smiles and double thumbs-ups. Streamers and confetti filled the air. My heart wanted to join in the fun, but my mind was dragging in the dirt below.

Still supported and held erect by my metal leg braces, frozen in time, I thought back to the moment that I got up the guts to tell my dad of that seismic decision of traveling to a developing country for an experimental medical treatment. I had played out this meeting several times in my head and rehearsed on my end of it while predicting *his* in a very somber, forehead curling tone. So, when it actually came time to living out this rehearsal, I would be more than prepared and ready to take his one final blow. But that's not how it went at all.

My dad misplaced his forehead curl just after the second I finished up with: "Stem cell treatment to help recover the damage to my spine." There was a shooting star's worth of time between the end of my shaky declaration and my dad's unexpected reaction. The lines on his forehead eased to show that he was really listening.

Everyone, I learned, was all-ears and all-walk.

It wasn't just visible in smoothed foreheads, but in radiant, toothed smiles and high-pitched hoorays. If those weren't telling enough, these gestures usually ended with personal check writing with the word "donation" next to a drawn-out heart shape in the memo section. People were not only wanting me to walk, but they were also trying to pay me to do it.

I arrived in New Delhi shortly before the monsoon season and in the middle of the night. I was fully equipped with appropriately cultured sleeved shirts (even in that heat!), vitamins and Band-Aids, a gigantic jar of peanut butter, and the excitement of knowing that Faye would be there to meet me in the morning.

As the airplane doors opened in the middle of the late Indian summer night, a swell of heat and moisture overcame me, as well did the aroma of things that I had never known before. It was a graciously overwhelming notion of the sweat of hundreds of bodies, that beloved garam masala, and fresh marigolds. Again, India had so many smells.

I stopped to take a mental picture. It was dark and crowded in the New Delhi airport. There were people in brightly colored sarongs and kurtas in every inch of the place, all going in every direction. I could hear cars and buses honking outside in the streets. I think I even heard a rooster crow. The swirling smells and sounds both intimidated me and fueled me. I knew I was in for something life-changing.

A calm man with soft eyes and no words was there to pick me up as I entered the masses of embraces, begging, and business deals occurring so late in the night. He held a sign with my name written boldly in the middle of it. The curves of each letter were swirly and elongated. We nodded several times at each other as he collected my things and ushered me to a taxicab waiting at the curb, under the moist night sky.

Whisking through the darkened streets of New Delhi at night was exhilarating and terrorizing. Zooming in and out of traffic—*was that a cow?* Feeling and smelling the impression of a world that was unknown to me, I closed my eyes to soak it all in. It was three o'clock in the morning, and this world was wide awake, taking full advantage of something wonderful and remarkable, I suppose. I just couldn't be sure of what, but I was dying to find out.

Arriving at the clinic, all but security lights were dimmed. The world outside was still bustling and honking, yet the world inside the clinic walls was fast asleep. I shuffled my way up the old iron elevator, knowing that if I carried even an ounce more in my luggage bags, I would have had to make a second trip. I found my room, shut the door, shoved my bags on the floor, and took a deep breath.

The next thought could go either way, so I forced myself to be proud of where I was and for the journey I had chosen for myself. I could have just as easily focused on the fact that no one could help me now, but there would be no gain in that.

Faye arrived early the next morning, draped in her own fabrics and smells of her current life in rural France, which she left behind just to join me on this journey. She had planned to stay for a month and return to France and the Buddhist retreat center she so loved. However, the second we embraced, we both knew that she'd be needing to rethink that plan.

Back to my current frozen moment of reflection, I caught my mirrored glance at Faye. And then to both Eve and Margot. They were all still, all with cautious smiles, standing behind me.

They were all there, there for me. I knew that each of them wanted everything for me. They were always there to stand me up before, and they were each by my side now. They would never understand, but that didn't stop them from trying. I felt an overwhelming sigh of relief, so much so that I think it shook the ground underneath and unfroze the world.

My moment was over.

Once silenced babies returned to full-faced expressive displays of discomfort, bladders were emptied, and photosynthesis recommenced, the surrounding world went back to staring at me while I faked several soft smiles for Dr. Mehra. Although I knew that she could see right through that prefabricated Mr. Potato Head smile, I also knew that it was of no concern of hers whether I was alright. She was going to get me to walk. That was her job.

After several minutes of shuffling feet attached to that Indian erector set attached to that American stress case, I paused for a moment before gliding downward, shifting my weight from my white-knuckled hands. I lowered myself down toward the comfort that I had been seeking the whole time in this suspension: my wheelchair.

Finally, this me staring back at me was one that I had known and understood for quite some time. It seemed that my years of longing to be just like the rest and wishing to go unnoticed as I tried reaching for things on the top shelf at the grocery store had suddenly vanished. It seemed that all those days where I searched for an elevator or a handicapped bathroom stall were now just a part of me. It seemed that I had grown. Accepted.

It was so clear that any sort of anxiety of becoming overwhelmed and obsessed with the trending notion of walking was nowhere to be seen. I was fine. Yet I was going to have to go at this alone.

Right there, sitting in the middle of one of the most overpopulated, bustling cities in the world, I had never felt so alone.

elbow-to-elbow with love

"SEEDHE JAO!" It was one of only a few phrases in Hindi that I was confident in articulating with the proper amount of gusto. "Go Straight!" In the month that I had been in New Delhi, I had become very accustomed to rickshaw lingo due to all the various daily outings that Faye, Margot, Eve, and I had ventured on.

This outing was to the pool for a morning swim. We attempted to go every morning, but as the days wore on and the summer's heat continued to rise, my confidants became far less enthusiastic about that routine endeavor. Air conditioning systems proved to be one of the most important decision-makers of our days, as well as that upper echelon of clientele that could also afford to worry about such necessary indulgences.

I can admit that the luxurious confines of overly air-conditioned malls did become more and more appealing. This proved even more true as our eyes became more and more open to the filth and poverty that surrounded every street corner, every food stall, and every hazed child's eyes.

But there was so much that I inherently loved about India. In fact, I think when I made my departure home, a piece of myself never even boarded the plane. I felt that pit of the withdrawal in my stomach for days, even weeks thereafter.

I loved and longed for the colors of bright oranges and almost fragrant pinks. I loved the care that was put into every spice and every curry I tasted. Yet, most of all, I loved the genuine nature of every soul that I came across.

Never in my life had I received so much help getting up staircases, opening ungodly heavy doors, and even haggling with the locals themselves for wares. Typically, I am so reluctant in my nature to accept help from anyone. Go ahead, call me *stubborn*. Jump right on that bandwagon, as everyone else already has. But for the first time, I didn't feel the need to prove myself to anyone. I also didn't feel that I *gave* the stranger anything for being able to help me either.

Something about the pure trueness of the people in India, living their lives in a caste system where it was impossible to move up in the world nor down, spoke to my character. Everyone was content to be themselves, their *true* selves. The Indian people could make no gain or advance in being falsely kind, and the notion flowed through their veins for thousands of years and more to come. They were not going to get anything out of helping me. Yet they did it anyway.

Finally, after refusing to be persuaded to visit a silk shop of a "very special friend" to our rickshaw driver, we had managed to continue on to the pool with minimal head bobbing and directional commands.

These morning swims were something that I eagerly looked forward to, amid much chaos in the extremely loose translation of "lap swimming." There were no lane lines—there were barely any competitive-type swimming gear to speak of. But you could always expect a full pool of locals getting their best workout in. Being so far away from home and all comfort I knew, I recognized those sunrise swims were what my soul needed to recenter each day. Each morning I was able to reset and focus on the true meaning and purpose behind all of my adventures in and around New Delhi.

My schedule was fairly open-ended. I would receive a stem cell treatment via small syringes either directed into my arm or leg each morning as I headed down for a long physiotherapy session of stretching, exercise, and "walking" in my leg-scaffolding calipers.

Once I had received the shot and the stretch, I would be free to roam about the city for the remainder of the day, as long as I signed myself out with the front desk attendant and as long as I was back by dinnertime for my next round of injections. For my twenty-something friends and me, this was pure heaven. I was able to carry out all the obligations of the very thing that brought me to India, all the while soak in some daily explorations, albeit in the middle of the literally sweltering Indian summer.

Faye, Margot, and Eve had made their summer homes with me taking turns sleeping on the straight foam pad they called a guest bed on the floor of my clinic room. It was so great to have all of them there to support me and care for me. But that same thing was also so hard. Rather incessantly each of them tried their best to show me that she was the one who cared for me most of all.

"I *finally* got us reservations for a hotel in Agra." Faye rolled her eyes with the notion that it wasn't her favorite moment of the day since returning from our morning swim. She must have been on that little disposable brick of a cell phone for over an hour.

"And the taxi?" questioned Eve. The two of them were the planners of the group and wanted to show their love for me by precisely planning out everything that they could for me and my time in India. Some might be annoyed, but having a well-thought-out plan for things had always been music to my ears.

Perhaps it was because so much of my life had been laid out by pure and utter chaos of my car accident. Or it was soothing to have a plan in the middle of one of the most frenzied and tumultuous cities I have ever been. But maybe it was always just a part of me, that sense of wanting to be on top of details and future upcomings. *Whatever the case, music to my ears!*

I was once told rather ominously by a chiropractor that my life had been suspended in the sympathetic nervous system when my accident happened. She continued by saying that it is the only way I know how to function now. My body was stuck eternally in verve. It explains a lot. She may have been on to something much more than releasing muscle and joint tensions in my body that day.

The sympathetic nervous system, the reacting "fight-or-flight" system that every one of us is wired with, typically only comes out when we absolutely *need* it. Imaginably, say, when being chased by a bear or a mountain lion. Or, in my case, in the middle of a midnight highway trying to hold on to each breath and large amounts of pooling blood.

Just look at my toothpaste tube, and that explains it all. Oozy and gushy with sparkling blue toothpaste covering the outer ring and cap. I simply cannot be bothered by such processes like closing the lid nor squeezing up from the bottom. The tube has lumps and bumps in all the wrong places. There is no time for such a frivolous effort. Having to move about my day faster than any sort of cap replacement nor pinch-squeeze can allow, my nervous system applauds me as I toss that oozy toothpaste back in the drawer.

Perhaps attempting to rationalize it all, was just another ploy from my psyche to plan and organize everything. I should probably start learning to accept that everything can't be held in the safety of your own two hands, put in a neat little box of understanding, and sent off to "*Plans for the Future, c/o Me.*"

I had almost lost all train of thought about traveling to Agra with my friends to see the Taj Mahal, when Faye chimed in, "Yes, the taxi is set. It should be here in an hour. And ...Dr. Mehra signed off on our overnight too!"

"What will we do about a car when we get to Agra?" Margot looked up from her North Indian guidebook. Margot was not only the most pragmatic one of the bunch, but she was also the most well-read, well-traveled, and well on her way to conquering the world with that giant brain of hers. Her blackish trusses that swept her forehead and heart-shaped face kept her both incredibly intimidating and welcoming all at the same time. Margot was, by far, the smartest person I had ever met. This sometimes made me left feeling unrefined and unintelligible about even the subjects that I swear I knew best. It wasn't her fault though, and god knows, she struggled with being the smartest in most of her social settings as it was. I think she often chose to date men solely on the fact that they seemed at least equally intelligent. Which, more times than not, made for an equally torrid relationship and eventual breakup. No wonder she would much rather keep her face in her book at this point.

"The taxi is to stay with us through the whole trip and take us home tomorrow." Faye had this thing planned to a tee.

"Hopefully, he's cute!" Eve was always the one to keep everything lighthearted and merry. I always appreciated this silliness and harbored a slight jealousy for not being able to be the same. Ever since I first met her in my freshman year at college, she always seemed to hold on to great successes, all the while being the most carefree and spirited, petite human being I knew. Damn her. She was just as cute as she was cunning, which always caused her to be bolder and more brazen than you would expect.

This, too, may be one of the reasons that my troupe of Three Musketeers there in India kept their personal connections far more professional when it came to one another. For having these three girls, my best friends in the world, come together in tight quarters for two months just for me, one might suppose they would all become great friends as well. It made so much sense to me. Obviously, if I loved each of them as much as I did, they would, too, have similar feelings for each other when it was all said and done. *Oh geez, daggers are forming in Eve's eyes, headed straight toward the back of Faye's curly head. Margot should really look up from her travel guide. Who is going to fight to take my wheelchair apart when we get to the taxi this afternoon?*

As much as I loved each of them with my whole heart, there were times I loved none of them when we were all together—and I hated myself for that.

That afternoon we stood in the hazed and polluted heat of the city, awaiting our taxi. Not only was the sun blazing down on us at all times, but it seemed that everything underneath radiated heat too.

When it finally arrived, we all took a quick scan to Faye, the conductor of this expedition. With a hard gulp, I whispered, "Where are we supposed to put our luggage ... and my chair?" The taxi driver emerged from his barely two-door hatchback, standing tall and proud, and definitely impacting the hopeful illusion of the size of his chariot.

"Hello, my name is Sanmeet. It means joyful in Punjab. I am to take you to Agra." And Eve was right. He was cute. Cute in that he-may-have-an-extra-tooth-sticking-out-of-his-hard-palate-but-we-don't-see-it sort of way.

"Namaste, Sanmeet. Could you open up the trunk for us?" Faye was just as curious as I was about how we were all going to fit in this car. Sanmeet, with his lengthy femurs and elon-gated everything else, was barely suitable for that vehicle, let alone the addition of four overly packed American girls and one wheelchair. I'm sure to onlookers we were quite a sight, yet as I scanned the streets preparing my embarrassment, no one seemed to even stop to glance.

"It's supposed to rain later this afternoon, no?" My voice cracked as I tried desperately not to make any one specific party feel bad about the notion.

"Yes, Miss. It's monsoon season, Miss." Yes, I was well aware. Sanmeet kept nodding his head in a way that made my head join in as well. I smiled a slight smile, as it was the only kind I could generate. He had no idea what I was getting at here.

After thirty whole minutes of stuffing and shuffling, we were able to manage each of our bags in the back hatch of the car, and one very loose rope wrapped in and out and in again around my wheelchair. Sanmeet had taken care to place my wheelchair gently on top of his miniaturized clown car, and I appreciated that. However, it didn't seem to diminish the fret that my wheelchair was strapped on top of a car with some rope in the first place.

That rope was the only thing to keep this trip from being a total disaster. That rope was going to potentially determine what the remainder of my time in India would be like. What on earth would happen to me, to everyone, if that wheelchair flew off the top of that car? Would it shatter to pieces or simply bumble on the ground just enough to be unusable?

I couldn't even imagine my life without that wheelchair.

Did I just say that? I couldn't imagine my life without my wheelchair. The thought made me both chuckle and cringe under the sounds of it rocking on the roof above me.

Looking around, with one small sigh into the corner of the car where I sat elbow-to-elbow next to Margot—nose in tour guidebook again—we were on our way in the smallest car I had ever seen in my whole life.

The trip to Agra, although only just over one hundred miles, took nearly six hours to endure. If it wasn't for the double-decker buses with colorful bodies overflowing out the windows and rooftops, it was sacred cattle in the road. Or it was the men with their surprisingly aggressive monkeys demanding money for those little vagrants to dance situated at every stop we made. *Why are we stopping again?* I was just barely comfortable in the clinic in New Delhi, and now I was in the middle of what felt like the savage of rainbow-colored, theatrical savages. I spent most of the ride with my head cocked, looking out the window at all that was displayed for me in each of those one hundred miles. There was so much rich culture that I understood none of, and it made me both sad and scared. I will never quite know if I was supposed to be in awe by the monkey or be incredibly petrified. Truthfully, I was both.

Every so often, when my eyes were sore from the stimuli and my mind was weary from the translation of it all, I would try to focus on the things inside of the car. Turns out, that ridiculously small car felt ridiculously comfortable sandwiched around all three of my favorite people, and one half-sexy Punjab driver.

Once we arrived in Agra, I somewhat foolishly expected the terrain or the poverty to change. To my surprise and utter shock, as we turned down the first town street toward our hotel, I witnessed something that my eyes could barely explain to my brain. There in the middle of the street, a small girl, of no more than ten years old pulled up her beaten and ragged dress to squat and defecate right there in the middle of everything. The home of the majestic Taj Mahal, analogous to a toilet for some.

The rain had begun nearly two hours before, and I finally forced myself to forget about my wheelchair. Wet is wet, no matter if it is for twenty minutes or two full hours. Sanmeet dropped us off at the foot of our hotel, which pleasantly appeared to be a little more updated than those surrounding it. That is, except for that gigantically beautiful, marbled staircase leading you to the front lobby. Most people would have 'oohed' and 'ahhed' over such an immaculate staircase. I just cringed subtly into that same corner of the car seat I was now reserving for sighs and scared breaths held in from the six-hour car ride.

With the rain bursting out its clouded seams, my three friends put on their smiles and pulled me up twelve giant marbled, and incredibly slippery stairs to our shelter for the night. Those smiles are ones I will never forget.

The next morning was early and full of anticipation of seeing the Taj Mahal. This was something that each of us had planned to visit during our journey that led us to New Delhi. How could you come to India and not see one of the newly established wonders of the world?

Situated amid filth and feces, poverty and pollution, is one of the greatest odes to love that anyone could possibly imagine. The Taj Mahal was built by an old emperor simply to house the body of this deceased wife. With such purposeful detail and mindful honor, this emperor obviously knew a thing or two about love and loss. The soft, white marble of the structure forced its way straight through the dust and pollution that regularly stained my eyes. The rounded edges and inlays of the building were massive, yet unobtrusive. As we ventured closer to the detail of this wonder, the love became clearer, as did this remarkable marvel.

There was a small water-filled canal that followed the length of the path, giving way to the most majestic reflection I have ever seen in my life. I made sure not to ruin it with my own, so I pushed my chair far enough toward the opposite side of the path. I couldn't interrupt this beauty.

When we approached the Taj, my muffled sighs returned as I realized I would not be able to go in. My friends were wonderful encouragers with smiles that said, "Yes! We can do it!" However, knowing the smoothness of such a terrain from the night before, coupled with the fact that you aren't even allowed to wear shoes inside, I elected to stand watch of my companions' footwear for the time being.

Reluctantly, Faye, Eve, and Margot all removed their shoes and headed inside the Taj, leaving me with some well-needed alone time with the other hundreds of tourists among me. However long or brief, I will never be certain. I took in the beauty that stood before me. I sat and thought about the constructor, the emperor, of this fine palace. Although unsure of how remarkable this emperor actually was, I could still admire him for his efforts. This wonder of the world tells me that this guy knew how to love. He couldn't bear to let his wife out of his legacy. In fact, he had to make *her* his very legacy. I told myself to hang on to that idea of love, as I might want to remember this one someday.

The Taj stood there, with all of its beauty and love, radiating to everyone who was willing to spend the money to see it. Yet, just outside those red sandstone fortress-like walls lived a completely different place, inlaid with grime and mud rather than jewels and marble. Did that mean that the lives of those who could not afford such luxury could not afford the same amount of love and devotion? It was difficult to discern, seeing the filth built up upon existing filth in a land of jolting poverty and dismay.

But I suppose it would be naïve of me to say love like that of the emperor's could only be reserved for him. It may be something that is more difficult for others to understand, or even recognize, but love isn't created from marbled stones of wonder. It's not reserved for only those that can afford it. And love is most definitely not contained in reflecting pools or sharp minarets.

Love is watching the eyes of my friends walking back toward me. With bare feet and the notion that I wasn't missing out on anything at all. "That was so boring!" They all chortled in unison.

No biggie, not in the least.

That's love.

said the spider

THERE ARE SOME THINGS IN LIFE that you hardly notice at all until you don't have them anymore. There is no prejudice, as they can be of any sizeable amount. They can be simple things, and they can be monsters of things. Moments like running out of the colored milk in your fruity, flaked cereal or running out of overpriced gasoline in your underpriced car. Those are simple things that you don't genuinely think about until they are gone. When they are gone, that's when they feel important.

So then take the bigger things—the relationships, the careers. Those things are felt even more when they are gone. But there is one thing that you cannot ever get over, there is nothing to make you whole again if you don't have it.

That something is your health.

Now you scoff and try to make arguments for why that simply isn't the most important thing, but I will win every single time. I win because I know exactly what it feels like not to have any health at all. Not even an apple a day could save me then.

When I was in college, I bought a goldfish. I appropriately named him Squiggly Two Pineapple. He was a charming fish, no doubt. But I soon learned that if you don't take care of him and feed him beer in place of fish food, he won't live that long. The bowl would need to be cleaned or your beloved fish would surely die and need to be flushed.

One would think that Ol' Pineapple's sacrificial lesson would have reminded me to care for myself. At twenty, there were a lot of moments that I chose to take on and learn a lesson from, but only if it didn't directly involve my physical well-being. I wasn't keen enough to look out my window at the world and say, "Hey! Thanks for teaching me *that*!" No, not me. Developmentally, I was engulfing lessons of acceptance and regret left and right. Beyond that scope, though, I just wasn't there. But apparently neither were any of my friends who helped out with the flush either.

I was going to have to learn from those mistakes like everybody else.

Consequently, I spent half of my senior year in college in the hospital fighting an infection in my tailbone that snuck up on me in the midst of late-night studying and subsequent party playing. The misery of having to withdraw from my school during the last semester of my entire college career, leaving friends, apartment, and job behind, should have been enough of a wake-up call. However, once treated, I continued on as though it was only a dream. With a hefty slap of the snooze button, I slipped back into my slumber of both ignorance and denial.

Somehow, I managed to continue to hit that snooze button for several more years, skating through bacterial infections and the like, with little other than a few fevers and cold coughs.

That was, until it was my body's turn to take complete charge and let me know that enough was most certainly enough. I got sick, and I wasn't about to get lucky like I did when I was twenty.

This was my "Dirty War."

To historians, the "Dirty War" was named so due to its significant and extreme nature of torture and deceit. This twentieth-century civil war in Argentina was one unlike any other in either its history or kind. Thousands of people disappeared, and thousands more only wished they had. Uncovered was the realization that the Argentinean Government was behind it all and the root of so much pain and suffering. This caused many other nations to become involved in an attempt to care for that particular self-instituted ailment.

I was going to have to fight a full-on civil war too. I had never been so sick in my life. I couldn't even pretend that I wasn't or that I felt okay. I certainly tried.

This war waged began long before there were signs of any gun slinging or soldier marches. I was hyper-focused on my newfound love for teaching. I hadn't ever been sick, other than the sniffles, as a teacher. All of a sudden, it wasn't just me that had to sit out this time. I now had students and swim kids that needed me to *not* be sick too. My bubble was big, and there were so many people that relied on me now. I couldn't stop. I began showing nature videos in class because I simply didn't have the energy to speak.

For a week, I sat pallid and tired. I swore I had the flu and acted by chugging gallons and gallons of orange juice and Pedialyte to help wash out whatever that bug was. All the while, my body worked overtime just to get me out the door every morning. My heart ached as it pounded against my chest. It hurt to shower, it hurt to drive, and it even hurt just to smile. I was in a bad state and trying desperately to tell myself that I wasn't.

As soon as the last school bell rang on one Friday afternoon, I hit the eject button on the VCR, and loaded up a cardboard box of all the things I would need for the next few weeks. There was little optimism as I headed out the door to lie in bed for eternity. On my way home, stoplights seemed to linger longer than normal as my heart raced. *I can do it ... I can make it ...* Just a few more miles and then the softness of my pillow and a few thousand blankets to cover my raging fever. I had been sick, so sick before, but this felt far worse.

Once home, the labored smile of mine drastically faded as I fell in bed, only to uncover the battle that had been carrying on underneath for the past week. It had finally arrived at the frontline, in an equally brilliant scarlet and balmy display of swollen defeat of my skin. My entire backside was red, hot, and oozy. Tissue from far underneath was exposed and crying out for help.

The infection had marched straight out of its origin and reached through to my bloodstream. I couldn't fake it anymore. This battle was going to take some reinforcements. I knew that much.

With little hope and even less energy, I closed my eyes to sleep. This would have to wait until the morning. Surely, it would be better in the morning. Life seems to always be better in the morning. As my eyes flitted to commence a world of slumbered fantasy, I focused on all the things I love about morning. *Sunrises ... brisk dew ... songbird prose ... that first awakened breath ...*

As morning came, I rushed to the only Urgent Care facility in town that was kind enough to be open on a Saturday morning. They quickly realized that this was no squirt gun battle we were dealing with. This *was* a full-on war, a dirty civil war with my body. No aid in the world could come to me quick enough, and I was hooked up to some IV medication and prescribed to lie in bed until further notice to see if my body could wage it on its own.

I had been on bed rest before, so I wasn't initially too depressed. Now I was hurting from all of my insides and being medicated by some of the toughest antibiotics enough to strip my veins as they flowed from needle to vessels. I knew right away that this could be a long season of unrest. I kept my everything-must-be-scheduled side quiet as I tried to focus on how great some rest was going to be.

After the antibiotics soaked deep within my body and seized up some of those nasty bacteria, I was able to venture out of my denial and finally grasp the situation that lay in front of me, or rather inside of me. As the medicine worked its sorcery, I felt better instantly. Yet, this was less comforting to me, because I had so much more to deal with than the infection alone. That infection had devastated nearly all the tissue, from skin to muscle and even bone. All of that devastation needed time to heal, and it needed my cooperation. I needed to stay off of it until it all healed. My butt looked like a forbidding cave. I couldn't look at it anymore. The sight made my eyes water and my heart cry for the fact that I can't even feel such wreckage.

Almost instantaneously, I was overcome. Overcome by feelings of terror and sorrow mostly, but also by a newer emotion that I had only granted access to since my early adulthood: anger.

Growing up, I never processed events through anger, I found emotions like guilt and confusion more comforting. My accident should have automatically given me the official rights to anger, but there wasn't ever the time. Nor the place. Those reasons usually had specific names, and those were usually people that also shared my last name. Lacking room for anger then, because I was dealing with my family, I had all the time in the world on my hands now. Alone. I planned it that way in my solo retreat house up in the mountains. This made it the perfect time to now include anger in my life.

I was stuck in my bed, in my home.

Alone.

And although I had consciously created a bedroom of color and light, my vision turned to something more resembling sepia, than the rich turquoise walls of my intentionally bold bedroom walls.

They instructed me to stay in bed, but how was I to do that when I most obviously needed to eat and excrete, for lack of more glorified visions? The influx of visitors to my side also caused me unnecessary grief. I knew they meant well, but it was the fact that they could come and go as they liked and had no understanding of the full weight of my situation that infuriated me. I wasn't going anywhere anytime soon, and we all knew it. There was no reason to smile amid your freshly baked pity-muffins.

This mysterious infection that loved me so dearly that it crept around, virtually unseen by doctors, kept me in bed for months. Eight months.

I no longer taught any students.

I no longer drove any car.

I no longer microwaved any frozen burritos.

I no longer exercised any muscles.

I no longer wore any shoes.

I no longer felt any sunshine.

I no longer looked in the mirror.

I no longer wanted any visitors.

I no longer felt like a person anymore.

I no longer smiled.

I no longer knew why I cried.

Certainly, it was one thing to be stuck in bed during an illness, but it was another thing not to have any inkling of when that sort of madness would cease. I felt crazy, like really crazy—tie-me-up-to-the-bedpost-and-spoon-feed-me-oatmeal-while-I-chant-"Cuckoo!" sort of crazy. I no longer *felt* ill, which was far worse.

I spent most days streaming tears of unrest, staring desperately at the ceiling, questioning a spider that crept across the irregularly bumped terrain overhead. He was slight, yet mighty as he spun an unassuming web in the ceiling corner above me. That precious spider stayed with me for hours and days. I watched his web grow. He knew exactly what I was going through. He was thoughtful and sympathetic and listened to my every word. The spider would be the only one that could both understand and encourage me. I spoke to him in the darkness about the things that I was missing out on and those other things that I missed most.

I would talk for hours about past regrets of effort, or lack therein. I would share with the spider the intricacies of my psyche in a way that I could never with anyone else. He was my friend, and he understood me, when I felt that nobody else did.

However, it was one shadowed spring evening, just as the sun was making its final descent on the day, that the spider decided it was his turn to speak up. Before that, he had never spoken a word.

"Get over it!" Came a haunting declaration from above. Confused, I looked around the dimness, to everything I could in the periphery of my limited view. There was clearly no one around, even in those shadows of the pending night. I squinted and rubbed my eyes. My eyes were puffy and clammy. My skin felt old and disgruntled. It felt forgotten and sad.

"That's right. YOU! Down there! You've had some time now to mourn and act the part of a loose cannon, but that's over now. Missy, you're done." Again, I couldn't focus my eyes on the voice from above, but I was frightened to admit what was actually occurring there in my little private hospital-grade bedroom.

It was the spider.

"I've been listening to you whine and cry for months now, but you have to stop. Your life isn't over, sweetheart. Life's just beginning. Take it from me!"

Only in moments of great sadness and vulnerability can one truly realize and appreciate the life that they are given. It was in that moment, there in the darkness with the help of a spider, that I realized something about life. I will never precisely be able to explain in words or metaphors or charades. To put it simply, I remembered how to live.

My life was waiting for me, patiently, somewhere outside of my own self-pity and loathing. It was going to wait forever, if it needed to. My life wasn't going to begin anew until I was ready for it. Laying there in that bed, no matter how horrible I felt—it was far more horrible not to even try.

From that point on, I took my focus off of the daily depression of what I was missing by being in bed, and began turning my focus elsewhere. I spent my days dreaming about experiences that I thrived and people that I admired. Nights writing and creating "to do" lists for both present and future. I swallowed hard on the notion that my health was going to forever be both more important and more traumatic than most. I accepted that.

Within a few weeks, I stopped chatting it up with the spider. I began speaking to my heart.

And, then one day, without warning, he was gone altogether. I didn't even get the chance to thank him.

The spider helped me understand the power and privilege that lay before me—no matter my current state, I turned my focus to just that. Bed rest became a way for me to see my life for just what it was and make different decisions about just what I wanted it to be.

I was forced out of it in order to get back into it.
To go beyond it.

For the first time, I could pronounce my full appreciation for putting my life on hold, just to have the power to reevaluate its direction and make changes where it was needed. I had made conscious decisions for change, albeit incredibly weak and uncertain about moving forward. The notion of finding and initiating those changes, energized me. I was ready to take those lessons from my spider friend and apply them to my life that was at its current standstill.

As for the spider, I never saw him again. Sometimes I would whisper for him after a full day of *living* from bed. I wanted to share with him just what I had made and accomplished for the day. I'm certain he'd be proud of me. I was proud of me.

"Hey ... spider? Hey ... you there? I just wanted to thank you again, that's all." He never did answer though. I was on my own and that was okay. Alone.

secret swim serenity serum

EARLY ONE MORNING, just as the dawn was breaking through the ignored and dusted windows of my bedroom, the light shone upon my eyelids as the only alarm I needed those days. Wiping and twisting my fists over my eyeballs, I felt a magical beat to my heart for the first time since I had landed in that bed well over half of a year ago.

I'm going to do it today.

I am going to go swim.

Shhhhhh.

I had to hush that side of me that had to follow all the rules. I was going to be okay with breaking the rules. In fact, it felt really stinking good.

The instructions were clear: Strict bed rest. No sitting in the wheelchair. Drive sitting on a cushioned pad, and only when going to doctor's appointments. Stay in bed. Stay miserable.

I had followed these demands to a tee for so long and had never planned on deviating from them. With a smile that felt so foreign and long-lost, I sat straight up in bed, feeling the weight of my body as I pushed against the bed in a way that my muscles had nearly forgotten. I had taken sitting up for granted. I had taken so many things for granted.

There, my proverbial road less traveled was in front of me. It was glittery and gold and filled with chlorine. It had been so many months stuck in that bed. So much time and energy to heal. So much time and energy that felt *lost*. I just knew this was the absolute most important thing in the world at my very moment.

I stretched my neck long and to the side a few times, to bring me back to my current reality. This wasn't just a daydream. My plan was in full-swing as I sifted through a pile of swimsuits in a drawer near my bedside. Finally, I found one that I imagined would complement the bandages I had on my backside the best. I was dreadfully nervous. I was nervous to be sitting directly on my newly healing skin and nervous that I was disobeying orders.

A memory of Adam and that one time we ran away and escaped from the hospital flooded my mind. Remembering my nerves for that day, I smiled at myself. I took a long, hard look at the full-length mirrored version of me.

Everything was going to be okay. I dressed in bed, raised myself wearily into my chair, and was out the door.

The morning air was brisk and nearly took my breath away. However, it could have just been a swirling mixture of the fresh, mountain pine air that I had been so missing and the desper-ate desire to be among the living. I gently piled myself and my wheelchair into the car. The sun was so bright. I didn't remember it being that bright. It almost hurt. *Don't keep that light out. You need that light. Take in all that light.*

Sitting very proper atop of my new hospital-grade cushion, I made my way down the hill to the gym where I had been allowing myself to pay for each month as I lay nearly motionless in bed. I parked the car and giggled at myself, thinking that this would make a very clever intro to a movie. I always thought about that when I was driving in the car with the radio on. Somehow, my movie about my life always seemed to begin with me driving somewhere with the radio blaring.

Looking around the parking lot, everything seemed so surreal. So simple, yet so complicated. It had been so long since I had talked to strangers. It had been so long since I smelled things like exhaust, blooming flowers, sweaty men, and bulk hand soap.

Just like many instances in my life where I took a little leap onto an unmarked path, my plan wasn't without its flaws. I gave little thought to whether I would be able to get myself in and out of the pool on my own, but I also didn't mind the challenge.

I was prepared to be unprepared.

When forced into a situation, it's amazing how many times you can push yourself to come out on top. Even when you don't have a plan. *I want to remember that one. Take a minute. Take a picture. Remember that.*

The pool was completely empty, save a few men massaging their own aches and pains away in the misty hot tub. They seemed not to notice me, which gave me both a sense of relief and great angst. I suppose they didn't have my background. They weren't going to stop me from getting in the pool, much in the same way they weren't about to applaud me either.

I situated my swim bag nearest the pool steps, laid out my towel, undressed down to my suit, and lowered myself onto the first step. Thank goodness for those memories your muscles hold on to and show up when you most need them. I took an elongated breath in, in part to prepare to lower myself in the pool, and in part to truly acknowledge the value in this particular leap. *You've got this. Jump in …*

Those first few strokes were chilled and so foreign, as were the breaths that came in almost melodic dissonance. But I kept on. I paid more attention to the water trickling on my fingertips as I breathed and the sounds of sloshing strokes more than I have ever noted in my life.

The world is brilliantly awakened for me when in the water. The dulled sounds that the water and its pressure create, lends to an immediate solace for meditative thought. That silence allows my mind to speak and my body to listen.

The water gave me freedom. For the past dozen years, it had been the only way for me to ditch my wheelchair, yet still feel wonderfully empowered. Suspended from fingertips to tippy-toes, the water held me up when I felt down. Its comfort and care. As I continued down the lane, counting strokes and paying attention to those now harmonizing water sounds, I closed my eyes and cried. *I was still alive.*

From that day forward, I continued my morning routine of secret swimming on the days when the home health care nurse wasn't coming to interrupt me with wound dressing changes and measurements. I mostly kept this secret from the world around me, because I knew that few understood, and I was so fearful that someone would attempt to take this new life completely away from me.

My blood could now pump throughout my body, weaving through my now-strengthened heart. I could see the color of life coming back into me. And, no matter how many times over the years I have tried to let go of swimming, it continued to renew and remind me just of who I am.

That blood that pumped harder each time I swam, I figured, could also take credit for helping my body ultimately heal. That extra blood, compounded with a new sense and quest for life. It was like magic fairy dust to once-necrotic and lifeless flesh.

It was a few months, but I finally healed. I owe it all to my secret swims. The very thing that saved me then, and continues to save me. Over and over again. My life always circles back to swimming. I can trust it will always keep me afloat.

PART
THREE

for certain

I PUSHED THE COLD, METAL BUTTON DOWN as I tried desperately to get the water out of the fountain faster. Perhaps I wasn't pushing hard enough? Or I needed to jiggle it or pulse it a bit to poke the water out of the stupid spigot? I had traveled too far and had too much on the line to miss my race simply because I could not get hydrated fast enough.

Faye had joined me on many swim trips before, but even before our departure to Bismarck, North Dakota (of all places), I knew this trip was meant to be something different. Now, granted, it *was* the Paralympic Trials of all things—the Mecca of swim meets for my uniquely damaged kind. But for some reason, I felt like this trip was slated to be so much more than that.

Something warming in my insides told me that there was to be more than just a swim meet. I thought maybe it was about that one guy that I had that thing with that one time. He would be at the meet, but I wasn't sure he was *that* special to me. I had trouble speculating, but my heart kept sending me signs. I think even Faye had started doubting all the whimsy and heart whispers that I was sharing with her. Unfortunately for her, it was all I could focus on throughout the plane ride there.

Faye saw how hard I had worked to get to this point, and I think that on some level, she thought it was absolutely ridiculous of me to transform it into something more. She had traveled with me to every single one of my races—plane rides from California to Canada, and back again. We gave her the title of "personal trainer" so that she was allowed to be on the pool deck with me, but everyone knew she was there to keep me going and lift me up (quite literally at times) when I needed her.

Yes, I wanted to make that Paralympic team. I had just spent the better part of two full years waking to an alarm that went off as most of my peers were meandering home from sweaty bars, dance parties, and unmemorable dates of all sorts.

I sacrificed so much, yet nothing at all. I wanted to prove to myself that I could train and go as far as my dreams. During one of my secret swims, I made that promise to myself. I wanted to try, to give it everything I had. To see where that could take me.

It took me to somewhere in the middle of somewhere North Dakota, poking a drinking fountain incessantly, drifting to wondering about the purpose of it all. Just moments before swimming my last race of the meet.

Faye and I had been here all week, even my dad had taken the drive to sit in the stands each day, the very way he once did when I was a child. He never tried to coach me, or even cheer—but his presence made me feel more whole.

Shoot! Now, I was about to miss my very last race because of this stupid button.

"Um, hello. I just wanted to introduce myself." Came a voice at me seemingly from nowhere and everywhere at the same time. I looked up to find a face. *It was that face!* My heart fluttered. I had seen it every single day since I had deplaned in Bismarck. It was almost like a game at that point.

He was unassuming. Had a strong-statured yet flowing soul. His sandy hair was cut clean to his head. I had noticed he chose similar looking shirts of blue and white, presumably from the team he was coaching. Each day he dressed the same, except for his feet. He must have really liked his feet, I thought. He put a lot of attention toward his footwear. From high tops to low tops to checkers to suede—this guy chose to display his personality at the very base of his being. I was instantly intrigued.

Faye and I had already pointed him out several times to each other, which wasn't very difficult because the pool deck was a relatively small, rectangle-confined spot to perch one's gaze. It also helped that this meet elected its host in one of the smaller capital cities in the country. Since there were limited restaurants and shops, everyone who traveled in for this meet kept extremely close quarters, including the chameleon shoe man.

"Hi!" I exclaimed, trying to force a casualty that was undoubtedly fake since I had wanted to speak with him since the very first time that I saw him. It wasn't the pool deck, nor the juice bar. It wasn't the barbeque festival. The first time I saw him was across that chain Italian restaurant eating with his athlete and mother.

But at that time, I was uncertain of any of the relationships at the table. For all I knew, he was married to that mom, and the swimmer was their bouncing baby breaststroker.

"I'm James." And that was that. I quickly offered my name, and before I knew it, my email address and phone number too. I wasn't sure what I was doing, but I explained haphazardly that since he was new to coaching Paralympic athletes, I may be able to offer some advice, or wisdom, or any sort of excuse to get myself connected to him.

As I finished my casual attempts at dictating numbers and letters, I looked up across the pool to see Faye waving her arms about. She was jumping like a mad person. *What is her problem?* That's when I realized it—I was up next to the block.

"Oh no! I've got to go ... uh, go ... go swim. It was great to meet you!" I pushed off across the humidified, slippery deathtrap of a pool deck, straight to the blocks of the lane where they were calling my event. It felt like I had already competed, my heart was racing with exhilaration.

On your marks, set, go ...!

That final race, albeit terribly distracted by James and the lack of moisture in my throat, I finished strong and proud. I had trained for two years for this moment, and I couldn't be more gratified. I had come so far, for myself and the idea to prove to the world what you can accomplish if you just *try*. All the sweat and pain, and all the strength and pride, brought me to that final race.

Just as any race ends, so does a competition. The meet was over. The experience was through. Exit stage left—it's time for the curtain call. No firework displays, no applause, and certainly no

room for an encore. I suppose I expected more. Never really thinking about what it was going to be like when it was over, left me
feeling underprepared. I never thought that far in advance, only
focusing on the event itself. As part of my training, I would imagine every possible scenario of the meet and my races, but I never
quite took the time nor willingness to consider anything beyond it.
I was always chasing *that* moment. I was training and sacrificing
each day for that moment. I was straining muscles and relationships for that moment. Even shoving all the money that I
didn't actually have into that moment. What I didn't quite realize
because of being so focused on that moment, was just that. It
was still just a moment. Like the subtle jump of the clock dial, it
was fleeting. And now it was over.

The next morning, we awoke to an assembly of all the
competing athletes, in hopes of hearing the same thing. We were
all hoping, with fingers crossed, to be chosen as a member of
the Paralympic Team. It wasn't impressive. It wasn't even formal.
The announcements were given in a small conference room that
could barely hold all the wheelchairs and canes necessary for
such an audience. No strong echoes for dramatic effect here.

However ordinary and stale the announcement, my name
still had not found its way on to that highly coveted list. Even
though I had imagined it over and over again, it still did not get
my name on that list. I could tell myself a million things as to
why my name wasn't on the list, but that wasn't going to make
any difference.

All of the athletes, coaches, and families that had piled into
the space, shuffled out of the building just the same. But there
were lives that were changed in there. Those with their names
on the list as well as those that weren't. Everyone that came out

of the conference room had changed. I tried hard to feel things. Although I wasn't sure exactly how I was supposed to feel, nor how I actually felt.

I had been worried for so long that I would cry if I didn't make the team. All of those hours in the pool, early morning alarm clocks, and sore and overused muscles. People were rooting for me and offering money and plane tickets to foster this dream. Was that time lost? Were people disappointed? I didn't do it. I didn't accomplish my dream, yet there weren't any tears forming. After blinking several times, to be sure, I heaved myself into the amoeba of rental cars, the most basic and rudimentary thing I had ever seen.

I closed the paper-thin car door as I waited for Faye to disassemble my chair and place it in the trunk. If I was going to cry, it was going to be now. But, alas—nothing. Not even a hard sigh. Don't get me wrong, I was definitely sad that I had not reached my ultimate goal of making that team. I had put my whole self into that dream. But perhaps that is exactly the reason that I wasn't more dejected. I sat there in the car silently, watching the world out the window in slow-motion, knowing that I had done everything in my power to make that team. Knowing that as the truth for myself, I had an overwhelming sense of contentment.

And, at that moment, a single tear trickled softly down my cheek.

It was for pride, not sadness. That tear surprised me, like most of my tears. They are such tricky stinkers. They show their glistening faces at every precise moment that I tell them not to. Those tears are, often, the only thing that tells others my feelings. Whether I wanted to or not. It is your emotions literally manifesting and pouring right out of you. Damn it.

But, for the first time, right then, I didn't care if they came. I was just focused on that moment and exactly how I felt. It didn't matter what anyone else thought, or even what I thought. Those tears were the embodiment of my emotions. And that was okay. My heart was speaking loudly, conducting my tears in a beautiful sonnet of pride and total contentment. I wiped my wet cheek as though to carry those tears to safety.

One thing that I know for certain about my life, and about life in general, is that when things are supposed to happen, they do. I have always been able to count on that. You may not believe me, but I would just argue that you have never allowed yourself the ability to find the necessary cues nor felt providence of such fatefulness.

My world and the way I look at it, revolves around this notion. Daily, my choices all lead me to some path that I was supposed to travel down all along. Sometimes there may be big crashes in the road, but those are all parts of a bigger lesson and a larger meaning.

Those things you do with your roadblocks,
that's what's called LIVING.

Faye and I sat in the airport terminal in near silence—some part because of exhaustion, but also due to that inherent bond of not needing to say a word to understand one another. As I peered into the overstuffed gift shop nearest our gate, I spotted two black checkered slip-ons looking intently at the carry-on snacks displayed neatly against the wall.

It was James. My heart waited just enough to miss a beat. I couldn't take my eyes off of that smile.

Without a second glance nor thought, I left my post with Faye and headed into the gift shop for some pretend snacks.

Without thought, without hesitation, without any worries to conjure up to keep me from making a potential mistake. *There he is! Here is my chance* ...I wheeled towards him with all the certainty of the world.

James caught my attempted nonchalant stare, and we connected over Red Vines and Reese's Pieces. I never wanted that conversation to end. He told me that he had to board a plane to Denver and then depart from his athlete, who was traveling up to Portland, as he continued back east to Durham.

"Denver?! But, that's my stop!" I remarked as I pushed on his chest playfully, and as to prove my disbelief. *It must be ... something ...*

We boarded the plane in a sequence of rows, where I led the way for all passengers as I always did. Using a wheelchair definitely has some perks. One of those will always be being able to board a plane first. But, don't be so jealous, because that also forces me to deplane dead last. Like, the-cleaning-crew-is-waiting-on-me-to-get-out-of-their-seat sort of last.

While on board, I sat with Faye scheming and dreaming how I was to coolly acknowledge James yet again as he passed by our seats. *Maybe he would be next to us?!*

In all my daydreaming, I almost missed his wave as he moved toward the back of the plane, the way back. There's no way I will see him when we get off the plane, since I'll be stuck waiting for my wheelchair with the surrounding flight crew, amid routine crew vacuuming. My premonition was sadly true. I tried not to show the disappointment on my face as I chatted with a flight attendant about the new brewery at the terminal. I tried so hard not to be rude, scanning the queue for James while I spoke. I missed him.

Feeling slightly woeful, pushing up the jet bridge, I sped ahead of Faye to find the nearest bathroom. If you are keeping track, that would most certainly not be a perk of wheelchair travel. Sitting still for the three-hour flight back from Bismarck, without so much as a wish to finagle the airplane bathroom, I prayed there was one close. I could write an entire book about places I've used the bathroom, and places I've been forced to use the bathroom because of the places that I couldn't use the bathroom.

Luckily, I reached the top of the jet bridge and located the restroom immediately. At that point, I had virtually lost all sight of Faye, but it was okay because she knew the drill. While in the stall, my cell phone beeped. And then another.

Where are you??!!

Hurry! Come quick!!

Oh, no. What is happening? Faye rarely texted me when she so obviously knew what I was doing. I fled out of the bathroom to the crowded airport terminal, looking frantically for my friend. Then suddenly, I saw her overflowing hair and reliable bright clothes up in the distance.

As I neared her, I realized she was talking with *somebody*.

As soon as I was within earshot of her, she smiled at me both softly, and so boldly, I could die. She simply said, "We are going to go get a beer."

"We are? Now?" I was very puzzled by everything, but couldn't take my eyes off of James, who was standing next to her. "But I thought ..."

"You thought wrong. Let's go!" Faye swooped around as she cut off my sentence. I was about to remark that I thought her mother was circling the airport, waiting to pick us both up. Perhaps she knew something that I did not?

Faye was always smarter than me, and I always trusted that. In fact, Faye did know something. She knew that *this* was my moment.

"Yeah, my next plane doesn't leave for another hour. And I already said goodbye to my swimmer and his family. And um, I don't have anything to do right now." His insouciance was in a do-si-do with mine as we walked down the terminal toward the shops and restaurants.

We sat down all together as Faye excused herself to use the phone. Obviously, she was calling her mother to tell her we were stalled. I looked out the glass of the restaurant walls and watched her motioning to her phone to keep those circles coming. From outside the duty-free shop, she smiled and waved.

I'm not sure I ever thanked her for that, nor her chauffeuring mother. But without that simple, single moment, so many other moments in my life would have never happened.

the ring

IT WASN'T LONG BEFORE I FINALLY made it back home, bags thrown against the floor nearest the entry. It was as far as I could muster. Such a long swim meet, and an even longer trip. All of it, a bowl of tired mush. However it was all the emotions I had been dancing with throughout that trip that made me absolutely exhausted.

I immediately sat down to my computer to scan for an email, or any sign of life at all sent by James.

Refresh.

Refresh.

Refresh.

Finally, like a magic tick in time, an email! A connection so surprising, yet so reassured. That instance made me grateful for that one guy that decided it should ding when you get a new email. Some emails just deserve that ding. And this was certainly one of those. Just an unassuming chime to let you know that someone thought of you just then.

The nervous and excited energy that flowed through my body made me dizzy. I clicked to open the email with a giddy sense of wonder, and a glass of wine.

Cheers! That was just the beginning.

James and I quickly moved from email to texting, and then from texting to phone conversations. It was so good to hear that subtle twang that he fervently denied on the other end. It was strong, yet unassuming. Only a few sounds had the pleasure of experiencing such a drawl. It was as if he had a very southern tobacco farmer living inside of an east coast pizza delivery guy. That combination makes such a sweet, yet confident voice. Unknowingly loud and strong, yet plunky like a banjo. Hearing that accent and voice on the other end of the phone made me flutter. My giddiness, undoubtedly, could be felt from a mile away. And I didn't care.

The next obvious step in our technologically driven courtship was clearly to video chat. Thank you, thank you to all the cyber gods who brought about Skype to complete my transcontinental obsession. It was there that James and I planned our "first date."

On the night of the big event, I spent the better half of twenty minutes picking out a shirt that looked nice, but not unprepared. I wanted to look casual from my computer screen, but not so much so that he didn't see that I was taking this as a big deal. As I tussled my hair in front of my video cam, I chuckled softly to myself when I noticed I neglected to change out of my twelve-year-old sweatpants. That, my friends, is the true beauty of video chatting. It says so much about how we live, love, and loath technology—all in our underwear and audio muted.

James called. *Phew, I remember him right.* We talked. *What is that photo of on the wall in the background?* We laughed. *Oh no, I really have to pee.* We endured honest pauses that were uncomplicated and never awkward. These "dates" soon became more and more numerous, and so did our plans.

We devised a trip for James to come out and see Colorado. Lucky for me, the mountains and cowboys and whatever else people from the other side of the country think about when envisioning Colorado piqued his curiosity.

We used our cyber-dates to plan out piles of adventures, enough to fill an entire month, stuffed into two weeks of let's-be-sure-this-is-real. And, as we planned, booking campsites, and drawing out the perfect routes, we both kept it silently on the front of our minds that this was going to be our test together.

It was clear, as clear as a new computer screen, that both of us were serious. Both of us were invested in this great unknown, and both of us were willing to leap to determine if what we felt was real.

His airport arrival was much anticipated. After all, it was the last place that I had seen him—aside from a pixelated version. I sat, alone, next to a metal bench brushing the front of my royal blue cotton dress. I smiled, thinking about all the sweatpants I had worn on our "dates" and how it took me so long just to settle on this dress. I put a lot of weight and pressure into this one dress. It had to represent me well. It had to be perfect. I had dreamed of seeing James again in real life—touching him, smelling him. I wasn't about to make my outfit choice mess it up. I kept nervously pressing out any potential wrinkles in that blue cotton fabric, surveying reunions of all kinds around me.

Watching all of the passengers find their loved ones, I wondered if possibly I wouldn't recognize James right away. Or that my memory of him and subsequent Skype confidant were somehow warped because of how badly I wanted this to work. *Did he have a big ugly wart on his nose that was shadowed by the video camera of his computer? Or was Abby right—did he actually fart a lot and smell really bad?*

It didn't matter. I didn't have any more time to worry. James was now headed right for me. I think my breathing stopped altogether until he approached me, knelt down and kissed me. Right then, I knew everything was going to be okay—farts and all.

I had been in relationships before, mostly with fear and no signs of certainty. I had nothing close to certainty with Wes. I always knew deep down that he felt I couldn't keep up, and that was a problem. I could sit in his sidecar for a while, and that was a fantastic novelty. Until it wasn't. But with James, it was different. With James there was never a question. I had to be the one to convince *him* that I could not, in fact, keep up with everyone and accomplish everything. He still doesn't believe me to this day.

With James eagerly behind the wheel of my car, I noted things that constantly made me smile. I immediately fell in love with the way he instinctively took his flip-flops off to drive, and how he took great care behind the wheel. We drove and drove and drove, for hours and hours and hours. We climbed over chilled mountain passes, across semi-arid and sand-colored land, and through old, greyed towns and romantically vibrant orchards.

After hours of driving, adventuring, and playing together we set up camp and drove into town for dinner and drinks. We found an old brew-pub that had TVs showing an Olympic table tennis match. I can't recall the countries, but it was perfect.

An all-brick interior, marked here and there with posters of skiing and drinking. It smelled of a place that the locals probably spent some nights watching football games and complaining about the tourists. A large walnut-colored bar took up most of the usable space in the room, but James and I managed to find a small table next to the adjacent wall to plop our dirtied, tenting bodies around.

Several somethings on the rocks and doohickeys in seemingly large shot glasses in, James held his half-emptied beer glass high above his head.

"Why don't we get married?"

Cheeeeers ... Wait? What? "Wait. What did you say?" I widened my jaw in hopes of mixing that alcohol quickly out of my brain to give me the chance of my best response to this question.

"I mean, not right now. That's funny! But ..." James' eyes were locked on mine. I could barely hold his gaze. I'm not sure if it was my heart fluttering or the alcohol, but I couldn't focus on him, on anything.

I'm pretty sure several dozen starlings finding their flock above us halted, mid-flight just to hear my answer. Holding my breath in, I stared right back. I immediately fell into his eyes—feeling like how Alice must have felt as she endured the rabbit hole. It was enticing and insane. So scary, so scary to think about. It was also so terrifyingly reassuring.

I exhaled all of my breath, rather intentionally. I was trying to calm down my racing heart and equally racing mind.

Like Alice, I was still falling, but it felt more like flying.

The majestic image of the Taj Mahal, of all things, came rushing into my brain. It was one of those snapshot memories that I encouraged myself to hold on to for *someday*. For today. I thought about that archetypal and intensely dedicated emperor. I lingered on that staggering, structural ode to his late wife. Reminiscing on the effortless marble, the inlayed sculptures, and the massiveness of it all. I finally understood.

I'm not sure I ever said anything in response, and I'm not sure I was intended to. That evening was definitely the start of every *thing*. And *everything*. James' Giant Canned Worms were opened, which definitely gave us something to talk about on the six-hour car ride back to civilization and my small mountain abode.

Packing up all of his belongings from my house, and from my life, I felt so much sudden sadness. It was all over. All the laughs, the joy, the discovery, and the pure excitement walk on a plane and away from my heart.

Finit.

How does a girl cope? We sat in mostly silence as James finished packing the last of his things, tucking them neatly in his duffle bag. My mind was racing, my guess his was too, as neither of us actually noticed or acknowledged the silence. So many thoughts filled my brain, I hadn't realized that we were sharing the quiet. But yet that silence wasn't uncomfortable. That silence was necessary.

The car ride to the airport was much the same. Not until we sat at the departure gate did I break the silence in my own disjointed, grasping for something I didn't quite know sort of way. And I fumbled at my finger, pulling and tugging at my ring. It was the only ring and generally the only jewelry I ever wore. And this I always wore, although it was a big old diamond ring in an outdated, gold setting.

It was my grandmother's ring. She had given it to me, my great-grandmother's wedding ring, just before she was too sick to not be able to make such a conscious decree. It was my most prized and guarded tangible possession, a reminder of my grandma and her love for me. It kept me close to her. Kept me safe. I never took it off.

Without a thought, I wriggled it right off of my then sweaty finger, and folded it into James' hand through the car window. Without a word. *I just took it off my finger and handed it to some guy that I had known for one month? What was I doing?* Can you discern between your honest reality and the things that you just really, really hope for? This certainly didn't make any sense in my sense-making mind.

His eyes perked up in both curiosity and anxiety. He glanced at the ring and wrapped it fully in his large-statured hand, as if it was recovered treasure. My heart pounded and ached as I whispered to him, "Now you have a ring for me when you come back."

He smiled and clenched his already-closed fist. And then he was gone.

beyond words

"HEY, DAD? I have something I need to tell you." I sat nervously next to my dad, shuffling the buttons on my turquoise cardigan. He was driving too fast, but that wasn't what was making me nervous that day.

"Okey doke. Are you okay? How's your skin?" He must have detected my nervous tone. He was now quite definitely driving over the speed limit. Perhaps he was nervous too? Although he normally seemed nervous, all of my prior health scares were about to do him in.

"My skin is fine. I check it every day. It's not that." Looking out the window at golden pastures and sprinkles of seemingly related cattle, I closed my eyes. "I'm actually going to North Carolina right now because I'm getting married."

To this day, I still don't know how I marshaled each of those words as we drove down the highway together toward the airport. I had procrastinated long enough and literally had no other option but to tell my dad minutes before departing on the plane. I was to see James and meet his family for the first time, as well as get married on their property. We had spent a couple of weeks planning the whole thing, yet I shared our plans with very few.

There was silence for a long minute, one of those minutes where you can hear your own heart beating, when time lends its utter strangeness to you.

> Time. It's one of those things that is so difficult to
> hold, impossible even, yet it is all around you.

It encompasses nearly every decision and dilemma of your day. And right then, time had swallowed hard for a full spelled-out-Mississippi-minute before allowing my dad to speak, "But, do you even know him?"

"Yes ... well, actually, no. No, I don't. And I can't explain it more."

"You're getting *married* this weekend?" Each word he spoke was heavier than the next. However, he wasn't going to argue with me or try to rationalize this decision. My dad was always the most rational, almost to a sickness, when it came to life's decisions.

I vividly remember a day in my early twenties when I made the very conscious choice to call him and ask his advice about what to do or not do in terms of moving beyond college. I wanted to go to physician's assistant school but was still a small child stuck in the body of a grown-up with Chinaware plates of grown-up decisions laid out in front of me.

I remember that day so well, mainly because of his response. Rather than walking me through those platters of choices and dreams with me, he simply muttered, "Life is about making ends meet. That's all." It seemed so simple and frank to him. Life was an equation, not an adventure for my dad. Life was a means to an end for him, and it couldn't have made me more sad. Those words have haunted me like the ghost of bad decisions from that day forward.

Yet, it was a different day. Those ghosts were suddenly gone.

"I am. We have it planned out. We are doing it at his folks' house. It's a log cabin in the woods. His sister and her kids will be there too. They ordered a cake and some flowers." Now I was rambling. I had spilled the beans and couldn't pick them up quick enough.

"Do you have anyone going?"

"No ... We figured we would do something to celebrate here when we get back." And suddenly, unexpectedly even, I felt the sadness in his voice.

Through all the cyber-planning and long-distance connecting, I hadn't taken even the slightest moment to consider what this wedding might mean for anyone else. I sank into the seat of the car and wished that we would move even faster to the airport. Yet, I also wanted to hold on to that unexpected feeling.

"Okay then." And that was that. I had just told my dad on the way to the airport that when I come back in three days, I will be married to a man that he had met only three months before. And for that matter, so had I.

We said our unintended-awkward goodbyes at the passenger drop-off area, grabbing my oversized teal camping backpack, buckled the chest strap, and set on my way to check in for the flight.

Luxurious things had little draw for me, mostly because I was too worried about the cost of those things, along with the fragility that seemed to go along with the description of such items. So, in the only manner I could find suitable, I purchased my wedding dress at a discount retail store just days before for eleven dollars and some change. I had it currently rolled up into a neat little soft peach burrito made of intertwined ribbon and tulle in the bottom of my towering hiking backpack. To me, it was the perfect thing I could wear for the day. It was form fitted at the top, with two ribbon straps, crossing at the back. It flowed out just at my belly, into a short flowy end at my knee. To hide my least favorite physical features, I had knee-high, chestnut-colored boots to wear, meeting the end of my dress rather nicely. I had shoved some matching costume earrings and a subtle birdcage veil into the side pocket of my bag. It was all accompanied by my swimsuit, toiletries, pajamas, and a couple of gifts for James and his family.

I didn't necessarily know what to expect nor plan for when I dreamed of this event, and dreaming about it always made me a little uncomfortable. *But every girl dreamed about her wedding day, right?* Not every little girl had to envision a wheelchair smack dab in the middle of that fresh blossomed perfect day though. That made it much more difficult to fantasize about. *It would look silly if he stood over me at the altar. How fast do I wheel down the aisle? And what about that big puffy dress? How do I keep such a beautiful event from appearing like such a disaster?*

Not knowing what to envision made my daydreaming much more stressful than I would have enjoyed it to be. I had never met James' parents or family before, save a quick wave over the computer screen. I had never been to North Carolina and couldn't imagine what it wanted to do with my natural curls and complexion.

James greeted me with his markedly long and open arms just outside the terminal. How his arms could fully wrap me up reminded me exactly why I had taken that very leap. I trusted the feeling above all else. His hands were soft, far softer than my callused and weary workers, and ever so gentle as he pulled my chin nearer his. I was exactly where I was supposed to be at that moment.

"Welcome to North Carolina," he whispered as he kissed me for the first time. It felt both so new and butterfly-y, but also warm and natural like a cup of granny's steamy chamomile tea.

The next few hours felt like a blur as we spent the afternoon attempting dating each other the way most couples spend years doing. We dined and laughed. Recounted each other's childhood, making sure to divulge any misgivings that we could think of. We held hands and embraced exactly the way I had imagined doing time and time again since the day I had met him.

Later in the afternoon, we set out for a swim together per James' request. I was glad to hop in the pool with him, although I wasn't sure we had the hour for a workout given our time restraints. After all, we were making up for several lost years of love and longing.

However, I was glad to clear my head and gather my thoughts with a swim. I really needed those in-and-out slow breaths right then. Stroke after stroke, I kept my eye on James and his "stroke after stroke." But, *where did he go?*

Just then, I spied him underneath me with his hand outstretched, holding my grandmother's ring. He couldn't possibly go another minute without a proper proposal. We both smiled at each other, goggle-eyed and underwater. It was Friday afternoon, and we were now engaged to be married—on Sunday. James was an old-fashioned soul in the middle of a dispute with a whirlwind romance. Neither side was to fully win.

I arrived at James' parents' home with more arms outstretched and smiles that were clearly of the most beautiful genetic presentation. Even the dogs greeted me with that same sincerity and openness. These people that I just met were going to be my family, and I couldn't put into words at the time what that meant to me. I came from a life where family failed to find strength and grace. I had often discovered myself alone and competing in a battle of some, table for one.

Somehow, James' family took me in as their own. It was like I had always been waiting for them to come along, just to find a spot to sit next to them on the porch. Rocking in chairs, looking out to the North Carolinian emerald woods, and reminiscing about days long gone.

With my awkward ability to isolate my feelings for things as well as my true character, I often came up short in new encounters with people. I didn't want to be like that, especially today.

Swallowing hard, I kept telling myself to *relaaaaaaxxxxx*. *Say something*. The introvert navigating my brain was not about to ruin this first impression. I had spent a lot of time and a lot of years coaxing that shy kid away, for there wasn't much room for her in my visibly wheeled life. I smiled wide at James' parents. As forced as it felt, it was an honest and true smile. I was completely happy to meet them and to be there.

James' mom greeted me with a warm Southern hug. His dad followed suit. I froze as I realized I didn't remember the last time I was hugged by my own parents. I still had a hard time even looking my mom in the eyes, as I felt so betrayed and hurt for so many years of her loaded, yet unintended selfishness. Flickering in that moment, I imagined that hug, and it hurt. I don't know why, but it hurt so badly. I shook that feeling off immediately and brought myself back to James and his family.

Of all the things that I had fantasized about with marrying James, I never took into account gaining a family. I turned away briefly as a single tear trickled down my face. Looking out across their wooded land, I paid homage to my own family of disfunction and misfortune. I turned back to this new family of warm tradition and deep-rooted comfort. The feeling overwhelmed and startled me, but I sent it away in the autumn breeze amongst the enormous trees surrounding James' family cabin home.

"Let me get you some sweet tea." James' mom motioned me inside with her long, sensitive drawl. And just like that, I was family.

"We have to go. You scheduled our marriage counseling for two o'clock, right?" James asked his mother. Apparently, other than being extremely beautiful and humid, North Carolina was also extremely tied to its religious sectors. To be legally married there, it was required prior to your wedding date to attend a mandated marriage counseling session with a church leader. Yet, as trivial and strange as I may have felt it to be, I was absolutely going to take this session seriously. I hadn't set foot in a church for years, probably since I was an early teen, trying to make sense of my mother's drinking and my father's frequent absence. *Would they tell us that we were fools for wanting to marry this way? Would they tell us "no"?*

"Everything will be fine," James grabbed my hand, pulling the car out of the gravel drive, as we set out for his parents' church. I squeezed his hand. It was my only response and that was going to have to do.

My grandmother was the one who taught me this secret hand squeeze language. For as long as I can remember, we spoke to each other in secret hand squeezes. And we always understood. Since my grandmother passed, I didn't realize that our special language could be revived through James. Until it happened as such.

We wound down a smallish two-lane highway, lined with tall green trees and the notorious tobacco fields James had described over video chat. Blanketing virtually every tree was a vine known as kudzu. It was an invasive type that was originally found only in Asia, but had made its merry way to the East Coast, and there it remains. Happy and healthy for the last one hundred plus years. It lined each road with its lush leaves, and I couldn't help but think it beautiful, invasive or not.

My fondness for the kudzu grew with every twist and turn in the road as we approached the nearly single-room church house. Painted rather intentionally in all white, its gray shutters stood out, even against the white steeple that stretched beyond the roof of the building toward the sky.

"We are here. You okay?" I nodded. James was busy warily figuring out where to park to allow enough space for me and my wheelchair to get out of the car. I scanned the building frantically for a ramp to get in. *Phew. James already knew how to look out for me without making it known that he was actively looking out for me. This, Mr. Preacher Man, this is why I want to marry this guy.*

We were greeted at the door by this Mr. Preacher Man, although he insisted that we call him Doc. Doc, was, to me, an unexpected man of God. He was casual and spoke informally of our engagement. He sat facing us with his body outstretched, asking us about our history. *Could you even call it that?* In firing-squad fashion, he shot off about all sorts of marriage hypotheticals, sure to stump even the longest relationships.

I suppose if I were to have to get grilled by a Mr. Preacher Man about what I would do if my husband disappointed me, I would want to do it with Doc a hundred times over.

Within minutes, I understood him to be someone that was loved by everyone. He had radiant, rosy cheeks that created a perfect platform for the kindest eyes. His questions were direct, yet unobtrusive. I felt like he sincerely wanted us to succeed together. And more importantly, he never laughed nor even cracked a smile when he learned that we had only known each other, and from afar, for the past three months.

"Do you both want to start a family someday?" Was one of his standard quiz questions I'm sure. Doc used no script and wrote nothing down for grading purposes or otherwise.

"What do you suppose will be your biggest source of argument or opposition?" This quiz was actually starting to feel more like the dinner that James and I shared with Faye and Margot, back when he came to visit me in Colorado.

We had the answers to the questions.

Having spent countless hours staring at each other from a computer screen, of course we did. In that specific manner of courtship, there is little to do other than talk.

After about an hour, James stood from the couch we had fused together on during our session. He shook Doc's hand and thanked him for meeting us. Doc knelt down and hugged me, saying that he was happy to marry us tomorrow morning.

This test felt much like one that I was sufficiently prepared for and I set the curve, thus being rightfully envied by the whole class. Instead of wanting to gloat and breathe in the pride of knowing I had finally figured out how to simply take a test without anxiety, I just smiled. It was so much more real and meaningful than that. It was nothing that I needed to make notecards or stay up late in the school library for. This test was *life*. This test was about the very thing I knew all along. I was so lucky to have finally met the one I was supposed to be with. It was easy, and for the first time, I knew everything.

I left that meeting more certain than ever.

The next day, our wedding day, was quite unlike most imagine about such a day. James and I took off early in the day to venture out for pizza near the Virginia-North Carolina border while his mother stayed back, fluffing and finalizing those things that she desired for her son's wedding. Her list included a proper cake, the best photographer in town, some champagne, and a few subtle decorations to make the homey event something to be remembered. Even though I didn't care much then, I'm certainly glad that *she* did.

Upon our return, James carried me down the flight of stairs to the basement to get dressed for the occasion. As I'm sure most couples do not get dressed together for their weddings, I'm completely unsure as to why. It was one of the most important and intimate moments of my life. Pinning my hair back as James folded his tie almost perfectly, our reflections toward each other in the mirror calmed me as we both smiled. There weren't many words spoken as we got ready, but there was also no need. He zipped the back of my dress, and I brushed his shortened hair behind his ear.

Once we were ready, James carried me back up the stairs again to the main level of the house. He placed me gently in my chair, as I patted and pulled at my dress, which was currently hidden under an old brown sweatshirt. The sun seemed to always be setting in the deep shaded forests of that North Carolina log cabin. My ratty old sweatshirt was going to have to do for now.

"You ready?" James knelt down and kissed my forehead. He was keen to know that this was to be our last moment to ourselves until long after we said our I dos. He smoothed his hand across my face, forcing me to blink hard in efforts not to cry then.

"I am. I love you." There was little nervousness in my voice as I unzipped my ratted old sweatshirt and set it down on the arm of the couch for later. James grabbed my hand and squeezed it with great intention.

This time, it was *his* moment for the hand squeeze. That hand squeeze brought my grandma immediately to me. I'm so glad she could make it to my wedding. I am certain she was happy to be there too. So certain.

With help down the exterior porch steps, James settled me onto each one with kindness and love. We greeted his family at the bottom of them in the dampened grass. Everything seemed to be touched with extra life today.

The towering forest trees swayed, splaying brilliant colors that only nature could provide. Sunlight swam between the trees and softly through leaves, appearing to illuminate them. The grasses, moist with water droplets straight from the air, glistened as well. It was all so beautiful.

The photographer began snapping away, in almost the same rhythm that I felt in my heart. Lub-dub, snap-snap. Lub-dub, snap-snap. There were smiles and hugs as we walked toward the pond where Doc was already there standing, with his sunshiny eyes mounted atop those brilliantly kind cheeks. James' family stood nearly still as they watched us make our way down the dewy grass. I smiled toward them, conceding that *my* family wasn't there. That was the time that I had truly chosen to notice their absence, and although I felt some guilt for it, I felt more sadness for myself for allowing it in the first place. While, a big sigh brought me back to my moment. *Our* moment.

Time began to slow, as it does sometimes. You feel that happen in two *very* different instances in life. On one hand, you feel it when you are supposed to be careful of the decision you are about to make, slowing things down to give you the best chance of doing right by the situation at hand. But then there are those rarer moments. Those ones that are so special. It is when something that your memory needs to grab hold of right away, copies each and every second of it for your heart to hold onto. It stretches that moment far bigger and greater than you could ever imagine for yourself.

I looked up at James. That time, for me, it was both.

one tiny package

"MAVIS. DEFINITELY MAVIS," I said, munching on a bagel, as James and I drove down the hill into town for swim practice. It was earlier than the sun knew.

"Mavis? Okay ... Okay ... I guess that sounds good. I don't know about a boy name." James entertained my thoughts a lot. I so appreciated him for that and smiled, as I watched him nod his head, focusing on the road in front of him. He tilted the steering wheel slightly right, then slightly left as we winded down the small mountain road in the dark.

"I don't know," I admitted bashfully. "It's fun to think about ... *someday* ..."

"We are not getting younger today, you know."

"I think about that *every* day." I swallowed hard on a bagel piece nearly too big to actually swallow. My throat ached as I forced it down. "Maybe now is the time to try?"

The rest of our typical morning drive to practice was done both in the dark and in silence. Not because we hadn't any more to say, but simply because those words got both of us thinking.

We had been living and coaching together for only a short while, but I couldn't have been happier. It is truly a blessing that our ideals and beliefs were as streamlined as they were, seeing we didn't have much time to dig up much dirt during our courtship.

We worked well together. We thought a lot alike, mostly. Those things we thought important as a coach to a swimmer, were just as important to the rest of life. That is one thing that made us work so well. It was easy with James. There wasn't a lot of added effort for us to understand each other.

Our conversation sat with me for days, as it did with him too, I suppose. And, if a conversation alone could get you pregnant, I would have to be more careful with words from now on.

I hadn't felt like myself for some days. On our way home from a swim meet, we decided to take our chances, and James stopped at the drug store and purchased the most reliable pregnancy test he could find. It said so on the box.

Crammed ever so gently in a bathroom made for one, we sat in silence—only this time it was because we actually had no words.

The test was positive.

And I was immediately positive that I didn't know if that was the right path or not. I started second-guessing my thinking. *What did I do? How could I teach a baby to walk? How could I keep a child from the cruel realities that I absolutely cannot do things? How could I force this burden on a child?* Maybe I didn't quite think this through all the way. WHAT HAVE I DONE?

Yet, because I had always been certain that life happened the way that it was supposed to, I had to trust that it was right. Those self-doubts weren't welcomed here.

I had to live each day this way. If I spent one single minute thinking otherwise, I might had suggested to myself that I was dealt a bum hand. Convinced myself that everything isn't cheery and great, and that bad things happen no matter what you do. I might have been a sad, sad girl.

So, I chose to look at life for the best. To simply clank my glass, rather than contemplate its fullness. That thinking had gotten me this far. But now I wasn't sure. Now, it involved another life. A life that I didn't quite know, but suddenly cared about more than my own.

The months came and went just like any other pregnancy, from what I could tell reading every medical website, pregnancy blog, as well as gobs and gobs of questionable forums on the subject. There weren't very many people who had been in my shoes. I was surprised, but also accustomed. My life was full of firsts. Firsts for me, and as far as I can tell, firsts for many of the crowd. Those firsts, though, they taught me about the strength in vulnerability. There is actually so much power in being exposed like that.

I had no clue what I was supposed to feel like pregnant, let alone pregnant and paralyzed. That word: alone. I could have easily been a Sunday night made-for-TV movie, with the amount of fear, follies, and frustrations. However, I made myself believe I had everything under control the whole time, choosing consciously not to look that fear in the face. There were no brochures, nor any articles, nor any information to tell me how to do it. I just had to create my own path and my own way.

I was following a path and also making it at the same time. Alone.

The last time I felt anything like this was when I was sixteen and just returning to the largest high school in the entire city, toting a shiny, yet ill-fated wheelchair. It wasn't necessarily the large ramps that got me, or the subtle stares at my legs, but something much more benign than that really got me: The fact that I didn't know how to wear my backpack anymore.

I wanted so desperately to be like everyone else. I wanted to carry my backpack nonchalantly slung over my dominant shoulder, with an exaggerated strap dragging downward as I walked. But I didn't walk. I didn't have the ability for nonchalance anymore. And there was no way I was going to strap my backpack to my wheelchair. People would surely see it then. People would sure think something about it.

I wanted even more desperately to fit the mold of a typical high school teenager. I had to carry that damned bag. Uncomfortable and lopsided, I strung my backpack around my shoulder, *mostly* like everyone else. It only took a few minutes for me to realize that it wasn't going to work. I was different now. There was no mold for me. I remember resting the bag on my lap for a brief moment before surrendering to hang it from the back of my push handles. It wasn't the path that I wanted, but it was the path that I needed. It was going to have to work.

One of the hardest parts about being pregnant was realizing that I behaved recklessly with my own body and decisions. It was always just me.

Becoming pregnant, carrying a human being inside of me, made me question whether or not I should jump that curb or swim in that sixty-eight-degree water. I had been alarmingly humbled and dictated by someone I had never even met yet.

Everything leading up was mostly uneventful, which was definitely not my norm in terms of medical needs. My obstetrician, Dr. Berg, had the utmost of confidence in me and my body's ability to grow another human. *Phew, at least someone did.*

"You're going to go full term. I just know it! You're healthy, and you know your body so well ..." I cut her off, this was our broken record conversation. I was at thirty-eight weeks, even though I seemed to be the only one worried about being so close to delivering. You would think that this confidence exuding from your physician would give you some as well, but her reassuring smiles only made me more anxious and irritated.

"And you think I will be able to feel contractions? I haven't felt any Braxton Hicks or anything. You know my stomach spasms all the time." I spoke every word without a breath, fearing that I wouldn't get it all out in time.

"You know your body so well ... so *well*. You are smart and intuitive. I think you're going to be fine." She danced her hands around the room as she spoke, like a kindergarten teacher or a puppeteer. Her display was obviously made to make me feel calmer and collected. Yet all I could think about was whether or not she was going to start singing "If You're Happy and You Know It" or not.

"But there is no more room!" I exclaimed, looking downward

at my overstretched belly, protruding beyond the scratchy paper blanket shielding me less-than-modestly.

"You have two more weeks left, and there is no chance of talking about being induced at least for another week. There's no reason for it, really. Everything is going to be *fine*." Her hands continued their dance, as Dr. Berg swept her long strawberry hair behind her back and smiled yet again. *Clap your hands, stomp your feet, shout 'hooray'!*

"I know. I'm just worried. Living in the mountains, an hour from the hospital. And, not knowing what I may feel or *not* feel ..."

"Nonsense, the baby is measuring just fine, and there is plenty of space in there. Even if you don't feel like it. We want to let that baby grow!" Dr. Berg was an enigma. She had a loud roaring voice, yet the manner at which she spoke was so soft and gentle. I wish I could believe her. *I wish I could get that song out of my head.* "Let's get you on the table to check your cervix."

Dr. Berg, in the most unintentional way, behaved more like a veterinarian than a physician with me. Moving with calculated, not gentle actions, I could only imagine her slapping a horse on the rear to get it running again just after it, too, gave birth.

Yet, her demeanor was warm and white-coat confident. She never appeared to worry about a thing. Propping my legs up on the table, Dr. Berg swept her cloud-like strawberry blond hair behind her back again, and began the exam.

"Oh. Oh. Oh, I feel hair ... Oh!" Dr. Berg melodically shuffled her way toward the door to the exam room, and gently swiped a conspicuous blue button, situated next to the exam room entrance.

"Wait, what?!" James exploded. He had kept quiet most of the appointment, because at least someone had learned that it wasn't worth the effort nor opinion.

"It's fine ... so tell me then, when did your water break?"

"My wa—?"

"Don't worry, it usually takes quite a while to get the whole process started. But we should get you ready to go to the hospital."

"Now? This is happening now?" My voice cracked like a storm coming from nowhere. A flood of emotions from excitement to dread had fallen upon me. Looking over to James, I knew he felt that way too. *Calm down. This isn't about you anymore.* In that same instance a soldier-like urgency fell over me. "Okay, I'm ready. Do we go straight there?"

"I would recommend that you work your way there now. You have time, so if you need to stop somewhere along the way, you should be fine with that. But, yes—you are in labor, sweetie."

I said nothing more, but what I wanted to say were words about the lack of contractions I was feeling or had felt. A nanny-nanny-boo-boo at least. And something snarky like, "remember that conversation we were just having, Dr. Berg?" Ugh. It was futile though. We were having a baby ... and now!

We arrived at the hospital with not so much as a hiccup from streetlights, nor weather, nor anything that could delay the most intentional drive of your life.

Entering the ER, I took a deep breath. It was that smell. That same smell no matter the location or the cause of bringing you there. But rather than feel defeated by that old familiar smell, I felt a smile start at the corner of my mouth. I lowered my jaw to not let it out. I didn't want to smile before I knew everything was okay. But this was the first time I had ever stepped foot in a hospital for a *good* reason.

Dr. Berg had called the hospital just after we had left, so they were quickly able to shuffle us through the ER and straight up to the Labor & Delivery unit.

On the car ride over, I had managed to send text messages to my dad, mom, sister, as well as James' parents. My words were nonspecific and non-urgent. The only way I knew how to send a text message about going to the hospital.

Lucky for me, my dad knew better and greeted us at our room only a few minutes after we had arrived. I often didn't give him enough credit. His soft disposition often challenged how I thought he understood me. I guess he had been paying attention the last few years, he does know me after all. I was genuinely happy he came.

My parents had finally admitted to their love loss about ten years too late and filed for divorce while I was in my last couple of years in college. Prior to that, they were roommates that despised one another. They couldn't speak to each other, and I didn't blame them. Splotches of sticky notes took over the countertops and cabinet fronts. This was the one and only way any successful communication could be had for these two married adversaries.

The times when I called home from college, I always anticipated calling twice. I would call once for Mom, hang up, and then again for Dad. And although they thought they were doing best by staying together until Abby and I were out of the house, there was far more relief when the two finally split. I felt so much sadness and pain for Abby, as she was stuck looking at those sticky notes every single day. My mom was sober now, but in no way reliable for all those peanut butter and jelly lunches she owed us from so many years ago.

There is some sort of lineage in our family of torrid divorce. My dad's parents had spent nearly his whole life running away from each other. In fact, I have a comic strip memory of laying in the hospital after my car accident and watching my grandma hide behind the privacy curtain of my medical bed as she heard the sound of my grandpa coming from down the hall. I'm sure this is why they claim that history repeats itself. Although, I have always been sure to stay away from sticky note communication and privacy curtain shenanigans.

The greatest lessons my parents and grandparents taught were those unintended ones. I could only hope for this baby, that I would be better. I'm not sure how I would be better or what I would be better at. But sitting in the hallway waiting for my room to be ready, I rubbed on my belly and whispered to that little thing inside of me that I would do my best to be better. *It's okay sweet baby boy. I'm ready.*

Once in the room, we were able to take a breath for the first time since James and I arrived at Dr. Berg's office earlier that morning. There were streams of nurses in a rainbow array of pastels with the only mission, to keep me comfortable. This was a far cry from any other hospital experience I had known before. I have spent hours in the ER, alone, with no more than a pragmatic white sheet to keep me "comfortable." And now I was inundated with warmed quilts and music, even framed pictures on the wall. This was *The Twilight Zone* for sure, and I loved every second of it. The sheets were soft and patterned, something I had never even dreamed of in a hospital experience before. I rubbed the woven threads between my forefinger and thumb and thought about how smart those hospital makers were to make this incredibly meaningful bedding decision.

I tried to remain calm and keep my thoughts on my linens. Turning my focus on the machine that sat next to me, beeping in my ear and letting me know about those contractions that I was "supposed" to feel. I sat, touching my giant belly around the cloth belts and sensors, "Wait, *that* is a contraction?" It was always such an eerie feeling when I experienced a moment that truly exposed my paralysis in such a manner. I just figured that I would feel *that*. The reminder of my lack of feeling was so chilling. Ironically, afterward people would congratulate me for being so "lucky" for years to come.

I tried to make sense of it all. But I had no time to prepare myself to prepare. This baby had plans for me and him, and it didn't matter that I didn't feel ready. That was my first lesson in being a mom. It didn't matter how I felt anymore. It didn't matter that I didn't feel prepared. That baby was coming. That baby was everything.

A nurse with a bright-eyed smile entered the room to adjust my blankets and let me know that she thought I would spend a couple of hours waiting, at least. I had let both my mom and Abby know that they didn't need to rush to get over to the hospital. Some out of the fact that they were both working, some out of the fact that they both inevitably raised my blood pressure. The reality was that my mom and dad made everything convoluted when they were forced into the same room anymore. My dad had a newer, wonderful girlfriend, Jackie, that also unintentionally made everything that much more turbulent. It was like an unexpected avalanche in the middle of a tsunami. It was *that* unfortunate. And, it was my new norm when it came to family. I accepted it all as it was, because it was *my* family. Learn how to accept and move forward.

"I'm just going to adjust your blankets a bit." The nurse's badge read: Judy. I remembered, fondly, a Nurse Judy from my first-ever hospital stay after my car accident. My aura relaxed a little to that chosen omen I put in front of me. It's a good thing I wasn't about to have a girl, as I might've had to change her name to Judy just in honor of it. My personal chuckle and deep-lunged sigh were interrupted by ...

"Oh, looks like you are ready now!" Nurse Judy popped up and out the door before I could even finish my breath nor begin a sentence to question her decree.

Within seconds, there were gobs of nurses in similar pastels, running around my room with machines and towels and stainless-steel tools. There were so many faces that I hadn't had the chance to even meet yet.

The pastel crew set up vigorously, yet in near silence. Their faces all told me the matter was "pleasantly urgent." A man in a suit and lab coat emerged from the hallway. He introduced himself as the doctor that was to deliver my baby. I shook his hand, full-knowing that I didn't care who he was, what he looked like, or what certifications hung on his wall. I just wanted everything to be okay. James and I began by following orders of the staff, playing it as coolly as we both could manage, for only the sake of one another. It's much easier to be strong for someone else. James held my hand as he stood next to the bed.

"Wait! Where did my dad go?"

"He went to the bathroom." James' eyes grew wide as he spoke our shared realization.

"That bathroom, right there?" I pointed across the room, *in* the room. I immediately imagined my little baby boy popping right out into that bathroom door just as my dad opened to come on out to see what all the fuss was. "Oh, geez."

I loved my dad, and I wanted him to be a part of my life and this new part too. Although, I definitely didn't want him catching my newborn as he flew out of me. I'm fairly certain that would fall under the category of "Things I Never Want to Witness" for my dad as well.

Somehow, with the pastel crew and their distractions, I managed to miss my dad sneaking away, Diet Coke in hand as he left the room.

It was only a moment, in a series of other moments. A breath. A jolt. It was a split second of everything and everyone that had ever been a part of me. It was a hummingbird's wing. The first drop of rain. It was a hand squeeze.

It was the whole of my life in one tiny package.

One single beat of my heart.

And, in that one moment, our son was born.

independence, together

AS WE WINDED ALONG with the mountain pass, the car weaved through small streams created near the road from the last of summer's snow runoff. The fall sun penetrated through the window and onto my shoulder, warming me slightly and preparing me like getting tucked in with a blanket for our little weekend away.

James and I had literally found ourselves in the middle of our dream jobs, only six months after we had gotten married. We were now wed and working alongside each other, and clearly together for the long haul.

I had been coaching for a local swim team under a stately husband-and-wife duo years before I had met James. When it came time for them to retire, James and I had found ourselves in their spotlight. We all agreed that the transition could be so smooth, as we graciously accepted ownership of their team. Talk about being in the right place at the right time.

I have always been so compelled by things happening for a reason. There is little that I have done or accomplished in my life that didn't feel like pure fate. Albeit, it has also been a defense mechanism for so many potential moments to feel sorry for myself. A colored blob of "you have no choice in this" was always much easier for me to paint. For, if I hadn't painted the world in this shade, I fear that I would still be stuck trying to understand what I did wrong when I was sixteen to deserve what I got.

Being sure of living a life that had already been planned out wasn't so bad. Just because I had decided that everything happened for a reason didn't make the really good things any less *good*, and likewise didn't make any part of it any less meaningful. I'm comforted by being in that right place at the right time.

We were in our third year of partnership, both in marriage and in career, and increasingly finding ourselves short on time. Suddenly we had no time to do the very things that we loved about each other in first the place. And now with a kid in tow, those seemingly mundane three-day weekends became the very thing that we lived for.

With the car loaded up with clothes and bikes and games, we headed to Aspen for two nights. We had found a tremendous hotel deal that was well worth this intimidating mountain pass. I was always a stickler for a good deal, and we certainly wouldn't have done this trip otherwise. I'm told it is my Scottish blood, that makes me so cheap, errrr frugal, with things. A fancy hotel stay in Aspen was certainly not going to happen on my end without some serious coupon-cutting and finagling. Maybe I'd even throw out that quintessential Indian head bob I so loved.

Aspen, set high amongst majestic mountains, was only a few hours from our house, but far enough and new enough to us that it felt like a true getaway. It was to be perfect for our small, adventure-seeking family.

"Did you remember the stroller?" I broke the calm vacation silence.

"I didn't bring it because he's been wanting to walk everywhere." James was right, but the little not-quite-two-year-old was not always the one that knew best. He was bold and brave. Defiant and independent. And the kindest, smallest soul I knew.

"I guess that's true. What a stinker." This baby had been growing on a daily basis to be the best of both James and myself.

It is the greatest human milestone I have ever known. To create a part of you, with the one you have chosen to love for the rest of your life. It is unexplainable. I had never known before how much I had been missing out on, floating around in my own single selfishness for so many years before. I finally felt like I had purpose in everything that I did.

It is so empowering to be a parent, and
the creator of such mirrored life.

It wasn't long until we were at the hotel, this brilliant chalet of deep espresso-colored accents and hints of lingering snow-drifts from last winter. We unloaded our bags and bikes, sans stroller, and headed out to explore the town.

Rows of boutiques and breweries lined the natural landscape of multicolored columbines and blue spruce trees. Aspen smelled like heaven—heaven in an L.L. Bean catalog.

One of our favorite times spent together as a family has always been simply walking around a new place together. Taking in subtle town culture with its unique smells and sounds, it's like stepping into someone else's moment, for a moment. I suppose I enjoy it so much as some sort of take on an unknown exploration, yet as a comfort that is almost guaranteed to accommodate a wheelchair user and a brave toddler.

Our smallish, loving family was built from the start upon tenderness and the connection to help one another. I couldn't be more blessed as I sat across from both boys at an outdoor eatery, nestled in the middle of the high-alpine town. We ate and laughed, singing 80's songs along with a brazen Bavarian entertainer and all the drunken patrons surrounding our table. Roo thought it was most delightful.

After the check was paid, we nestled back into the chalet for some much-needed rest for the night. Our Aspen getaway made it much easier to slow down and appreciate a sunsetting stroll down the street, or a vanilla soft-serve ice cream cone on a whim.

As we tucked in to bed, I slowed for a moment to recognize the love that James had for me. We lay there, two peas in an upside-down pod. Upside-down, with our feet where our head should be, making no mention of its absurdity.

I had begun sleeping that way shortly after we got married, as I swore it made for a better night's rest. Some sort of Zen thing, or even a magnetic episode. I'm unsure of the cause, but it felt right. So, I never went back. Nor did James. He just followed suit, never questioning, and never criticizing. He simply chose to sleep upside-down because he loves me. To this day, it is still that way, and in the heat of an argument the image of us flip-flopped sleepers settles me to soften the moment always.

I closed my eyes and thanked the fancy black-out curtains for my darkened comfort, and nuzzled into James' nape.

"Babe, your alarm is going off. Again." I tried my best to keep the tone of judgment out of my voice as James shuffled around under the covers. It was his third alarm already. It was partly that, and partly the jealousy that I knew he was about to rise to go out and explore his own version of Aspen on his mountain bike, alone. James' first love was, and will always be, his bike.

Ever since giving birth, I had lost so much of a sense of that very thing: aloneness. And not necessarily because I wasn't granted it. Goodness knows that James had given me every opportunity. However, being a mom was now a job that didn't have a switch. There was no turning it off, or even dimming that light any. I am a mom. The most secretly powerful job in the universe, and I wasn't about to drop it even for a second to indulge in something like exercise or self-exploration. James pitied my view, and—on some level—I did too. But nonetheless, this was me.

I am a mom.

"I love you, guys. I will see you after breakfast. Have fun with the little man." And, with the dawn of the day, James left out the door, clicking and clanking his bicycle shoes as he attempted a muted tiptoe in size 13 cycling shoes out of the chalet.

Appreciating that James often got lost in time while biking, and sometimes just plain lost, I made a loose plan that involved a well-deserved morning coffee, a wide-eyed almost-two-year-old, and an undoubted adventure.

In thinking that our adventure would be found just around the next street corner, I pulled on my ten-year-old, yet brand-new-looking-because-I-don't-use-them-to-walk boots and Roo's purple hand-me-downs. We zipped up parkas up to our chins, concealing our pajamas underneath. I grabbed for my scarf on our way out the door.

This scarf wasn't any old scarf, though. This scarf had magic powers. I had purchased it with a great deal of haggling while in India. I was drawn to its beauty immediately, and knew that it was worth every moment and every rupee of that half-spoken, half-inferred Hindi interaction. Made up of every rainbow color woven tightly and intricately in a way that made it appear as only a brilliant burgundy color from afar. It held subtle highlights of blues and oranges, greens and purples, and felt like a warm hug around my body, as if someone had fashioned a scarf for my very soul. It was the most unexpected and necessary of tangible things.

The comfort and confidence that this scarf has brought me over the years is something unfathomable. Thus, it was absolutely imperative to wrap around my neck as Roo and I walked out that door.

"Push the elevator button. The bottom one. Go ahead." James and I were constantly trying to teach Roo how to be independent, some due to our daily lives spent working with kids. And some in part to the fact that we were both well-aware that there would be instances where he would need to seek out an independence beyond my own capacities.

"Mama, let's go!" His voice was as soft as you would expect a toddler's to be, but yet with a tone that was commanding beyond his years. This Roo of mine spent the majority of his short two years being towed around to swim meets and the like, interacting with various parents and their pre-adolescents that unintentionally yearned to teach him something. Inevitably he learned a lot.

We exited the elevator on the bottom floor and stepped out onto the main sidewalk lined with a muted rainbow of flowers and alpine plants. The sun had rested on the leaves ever so gently not to wake their still slumber.

I wanted to grab for Roo's hand, but I needed both hands to push and direct my wheelchair, so walking hand-in-hand with my son was never an option. I tried never to think about it. That reality is one that deeply saddens me.

Mostly, I would try to coax him to sit on my lap to get from place to place, but he was quickly growing out of that way to ride. *This is stupid. Maybe we should go back. We haven't practiced crossing streets or anything together. Damn James, why did he have to go ride? Why did I have to need him?*

"C'mon, Baby Boy, this way." I swallowed hard. Swallowing my fears and my fear's fears even harder. I didn't want him to sense any of it in my voice, so I stopped talking altogether. *This is wrong of me. I shouldn't take him down the sidewalk alone. I don't trust him. I don't trust myself.* Tears began to well up in my already stinging eyes. *This isn't fair.*

Stop! Don't let yourself go there. This is life. This is your life. Breathe—you've got this.

The whole thing unmistakably took me back to my own six-year-old jelly shoes and licorice sticks piled in a red wagon clearly meant for my own independent departure from home.

My six-year-old-self wanted to run away from home and had every intention of saying "sayonara" to my Barbie dolls, my Little Tykes bike, and my parents forever. I have no recollection of the events that led up to my bold departure, but I was definitely serious about it. In fact, that little red wagon full of licorice was stubbornly pulled all the way to the end of the block by yours truly, when I reached a standstill in my stomach. I remember thinking it was hunger and headed back home for dinner, but looking back, that may have just been my first taste of fear and the fear that independence often brings. Ironically, I still take licorice on every road trip and adventure that I can.

"Okay, here is a new rule ... ehh, game! You have to walk right next to my big wheel and stay there. Got it?"

"Hmm, mmmmm-hummmmm!" He loved games and challenges and anything that he could prove himself as a "big boy." Maybe one of these days, I will stop calling him Baby.

"Wheeeeeeel! Wheeeeeeeeeeeel!" I called in a sing-song voice, pointing to my worn tires and scraped metal push rims. To my surprise, Roo did exactly as I had demanded. He stayed close to my back wheel, right next to me and my chair. He listened to my commands of "stop!" and "don't touch that!" with almost militant form. Step for step, I was realizing that this forced independence was perhaps something that we both needed, together. It would be silly for me not to notice that he already had a heightened sense of those things Mommy can do and those other things Mommy certainly cannot.

Checking the map on my phone, we turned right, then left ... we went up three blocks and down another. Checking my watch, we had already been gone an hour.

"We're almost there!" I assured him and both of our hungry tummies. "There, there it is! That white and grey sign." Squinting in the morning sun, I pointed to a small café tucked in a corner of shops and stairs, and one very important ramp for us to whiz down and enter the building at last.

With latte in my hand, and chocolate milk running down Roo's, we clanked our paper cups and cheered our adventure. Wiping sweat off of my forehead, the sweat of a thousand worries, I smiled at my sweet boy across the table as he swung his legs in pure joy.

I breathed deeply for the first time since we stepped foot out of the elevator. In fact, I breathed more deeply than I had since he was born.

I can do this. We can really do this.

And we will do it together.

to be a mom

"MY HEART DOES A LOT OF WORK. Sometimes I talk to my heart." Uttered the softened voice of pure innocence in the half darkness of the night. The glow of the translucent turtle nite-lite was strong enough to radiate against the other wall. It showed off hand-painted grass stalks of multiple greens, made with my own acrobatic maneuvers of painting so close to the ground from the height of a wheelchair. It wasn't perfect, by any means, but it quietly displayed the pure love I had for this particular four-year-old lying next to me.

"What do you talk to your heart about?" I whispered in a matched tone. I loved these moments so much that I wished to grab them with my breath and inhale them directly to my heart for safe-keeping. Throughout my life, I often told myself, "Remember this moment, please remember this moment forever." Those moments had enormously flourished since Roo was born.

I had hoisted myself onto his tiny twin bed, propping up both of my legs as if I were planning on sleeping there too. That's what he wanted at least. And each night, either I or James would spend anywhere from a half an hour to two hours putting this sweet, yet stubborn little man to bed. Tonight, was my turn.

"Mom, why don't you walk?" He sighed, apparently something he had talked with his heart about before. I sighed too.

I knew this day was coming, but I didn't quite know it was happening tonight lying in bed with him. My only plan for the evening had been getting this boy to sleep in the least amount of time possible, all while making him feel special for the attention and care in the process.

Being well into my thirties, chasing four-year-old curiosities, I was tired. I combed my hands through his mess of blonde curls, and equally through the leftover mess and dirt of his very sticky preschooler day.

Being a mom was something that I had always wanted, but never put too much weight on, likely for fear of never attaining such a dream. It wasn't until I met James that it transitioned from something I *thought* about wanting into something that my soul actually ached for.

"We've talked about it before. I don't walk because my legs don't work."

"How old are your legs?"

"Sweet boy, they are the same age as the rest of me."

"Okay, what about your arms?"

"All of my body is the same age ... my legs, my arms, my tummy, and my head. Maybe my legs look like they are a different age to you because they don't work the same as other mommies."

"All the other mommies walk and are tall." He often liked

252

to point out how short I was compared to other grown-ups in his life. I'm not sure he took the moment to realize that it was because I was sitting down, or if he believed that my chair made me smaller. Either way, I know that four-year-olds are really into size and age, and I wasn't going to be bothered by his inquisition. I had heard similar things most of my life.

"Yes, they do. Yes, they are. I'm just a different sort of mommy."

He broke in– "with two belly buttons!" That was something I am certain he bragged to his preschool friends about. I cringed a little, thinking about it. He was referring to a scar on my belly from my first emergent days at the hospital after my accident when they sliced a small hole, sewed in a GI tube that flowed greenish, greyish food straight to my belly for the nourishment to keep me alive. Thank goodness all that remained from those days for him was my super spectacular second belly button.

"Yes, baby. You got it." There was a long pause of silence, one that I have heard before. I thought I may be off the hook and that the sandman whisked this sweet boy away for the night to dream of those favorite things of his–swimming and school, naked mole rats, and his beloved teddy bear, Goldilocks.

As I too had closed my eyes, he whispered abruptly, "You were in an accident a long time ago ... but not when the dinosaurs were living." This concept is strange for even some adults to grasp, and now I was trying to rationalize with a four-year-old that I was in a tragic car accident that broke my spine? *Oh, baby, how you don't deserve this.*

In the past twenty years, I have been asked by countless children, with shushing moms and dads in the background, the very same question. However, this time was the first time that it truly made my heart sink to where I feared it may be lost beyond me forever.

As the years wore on after my accident, I became more and more aware of how my paralysis was indeed something carried by my loved ones, and perhaps, on some level, carried even more.

I knew that my accident and injuries far impacted my family more than myself. I think of my mom, who spiraled down with alcohol fast after her daughter almost died. I think of my dad, who didn't find any resemblance of joy, for his days were full-up of making his ends meet. And then there was my sister, Abby, who struggled, as her child psychologist put it, because her brain stopped growing the instant I was injured. Whether there was blame to be had, wasn't critical. What was, however, was that each sustained a lot of trauma from a car accident of which they were never even a passenger.

But now I was grown and making a family of my own. How could I be so stupid not to think that my new family wouldn't hurt somewhat the same?

I am so, so sorry.

No matter how hard I tried to live like everyone else, naively taking my existence for granted, I simply couldn't manage such the boring life that I yearned for. Who, other than me, wished desperately to be more dull for the ones they loved?

With my heart heavily pressing me to the bed, I felt like I could barely breathe. This was one of many times that I had realized that my paralysis and accident followed me eternally. It was so cruel that it had to seep into this sweet child too. He had no part in this life—he was simply born to it. At times, I can make myself believe that it is a good thing for him, and he will grow into a much better human because of it. In the same breath, there are so many other instances where I just can't force that positivity and it hurts. It hurts so much.

"I *was* in an accident. Good memory. I'm okay though and there are lots of things that I can do!" I always tried encouraging him, so I thought that this kind of positivity would carry him to help switch the current tone of the moment.

"You can roll!"

"Yes, I can."

"You can make me dinner ..."

"Yep, that too."

"You can wipe my bottom ..." Very important. Yes. "You can walk me to school ... you can read me books ..."

I was getting the sense that the tables had turned, and he was out to teach me a lesson, there in that darkened twin bed surrounded by plastic-eyed teddy bears and Disney characters. I think they were all staring at me to speak, but I just laid there.

"*Say something,*" whispered Goldilocks, the stuffed bear.

"You can give me smooches." His soft voice whispered. And with that, I thought I could no longer contain myself. I sucked in my heated breath, trying not to let twenty-plus years' worth of emotion out right then. Moving his sweaty, matted curls from his forehead, I kissed him and wiped a tear from my own cheek. "Thank you, baby." And with that, we both closed our eyes. Our meeting had ended for the night. Court adjourned.

Just because it was the end of that talk, didn't mean much. Roo was a growing boy, one of the biggest in his class at school, definitely with the brains to match his brawn. I would be silly not to expect more from him every single day. And he deserved that much. He deserved to understand the world as much as he inquired about it.

Just in the prior few weeks, he had started gliding his hand behind my wheelchair to give me a slight push up a hill, much in the same way his daddy did. He never made mention of it and never turned rogue, mistaking me for an Indy 500 car replica. He just recognized when I needed an extra push.

He had simply learned to give me a little help when I may need it. No words necessary, just help. I'm not even sure how you could teach someone something like that if you tried.

He took as much care of me as I did of him.

This softhearted boy offered me a life that I had no idea existed before. This boy made me a mom.

Becoming a mom changed me in so many ways. It is certainly no title to take for granted, nor one that should come easy. Just because someone gives birth to you, doesn't make them a mom. Through so many trials of my own—struggling with my own mom and searching desperately for someone to fill her place—I certainly knew the value of that role. You often learn the precise value of things that way.

Before gently getting out of Roo's bed and pushing my wheels quietly out of his door, I made a silent vow to him. I soundlessly declared to be the best mom I *should* be for him. I vowed that he would always know my love and never feel that hurt that I did so long ago.

It was also for my own self. I vowed to that sobbing-kid-version of me, who hid in a closet away from her mom. I've grown so much, but that version of me still lives inside of me today.

Although time had lessened the sting, that hurt would always be there. Every decision, every encounter, and every moment would have a piece of *my* mom in it.

That is just how powerful it is to be a mom.

There is one memory that has always stuck with me, especially now having a child the exact age of the recollection. The vision is a smallish and shiny, yet extremely ugly and brown handmade pot. Now, if you ask anyone in my family, it was mine. I made it in preschool and brought it home, just like all the other children in my classroom. Yet, I would have never made something so hideous and plain.

My pot was a beautiful rose color and the creases were all wiped clean over and over again by my tiny, thoughtful hands. I had always had a fondness for art, and I have always taken a lot of pride in all the things that I have made with my own two hands. Except for this damned brown pot. I didn't make that.

Somehow, in the shuffle of getting the entire class to take their pots home, mine was misplaced. I remember being so disheartened when I asked my teacher about it. She brushed it off rather nonchalantly, even for a preschool teacher, and tried to convince me that the poo-colored one was mine. Being extremely obedient at four, I would never have doubted a teacher. I took the slimy, brown pot with open arms and a forced smile. And then cried the whole way home.

In the same notion that my teacher brushed off my plea to find my real pot, my parents did the same. They accepted this terrible pot as mine, and I can even recall the stab I felt knowing that my mom thought I would construct such a foul thing, and not convincing her otherwise.

The memory is something so subtle in a world filled with brown, ugly pots. Yet, it is something incredibly profound when I think of the absolute impact that a mother has on her child. All I ever wanted was for my mom to be angry at my teacher for misplacing my pot. That would have made all the difference in my world.

The shadows of the room lay still and quiet as Goldilocks spoke again to me, "He knows. He knows in all of his heart all the things in yours. All of it is what makes him so wonderfully part of you." I smiled and closed the door behind me ever so gently, yet smashing that terrible brown pot in my mind.

i/she tried

"**OKAY, YOU'RE GETTING WARMER** ... warmer ... now colder. So cold, you're in a freezer now ..." I giggled as I tried desperately to guide Roo to a woven basket on the kitchen counter.

That basket was full of green and red apples, a few brownish bananas awaiting their ultimate banana-bready destiny, and a small square of red construction paper with the letter "A" drawn on it.

James and I knew as soon as we found out that we had to tell him first. Once he knew, the world might soon know too. We had been preparing for that. In order to engage and connect with Roo in a way to make sure that this was exciting news for him, James and I concocted a scavenger hunt of sorts where he had clues to find various squares of construction paper with letters and pictures to help spell out our news for him.

After he was born, I couldn't possibly imagine having another child. I felt so connected to this little human thing that I didn't see it quite fair to add anything else to our seemingly completed fairy tale. I was certain there was no extra love left to give.

In fact, I was so certain that we packed up gobs and gobs of baby clothes and toys, and gave them away to expecting friends. We were certainly not expecting to ever be expecting again.

Our family of three encompassed all the love that each of us had, that was until it didn't.

Something happened to me, to us, when Roo turned four. A switch flipped inside of me, and my adamancy for not having another child changed to the very opposite. I went from thinking it wasn't fair to add another child to Roo's life to thinking that it wasn't fair *not* to add another child. And almost as instantaneously as we decided to try for it, we found out that we were going to have another baby boy. A baby, again!

"A little to the side ... no, other side." James was rolling his eyes at how oblivious a four-and-a-half-year-old can be when searching for something. Living with a four-year-old is sometimes akin to living with a drunkard. He needs help constantly with making simple decisions, like breakfast. He can never find his shoes. Forgets to close the refrigerator door. His shoes are in the refrigerator. Moreover, he can't ever find that one thing he is looking for right in front of him.

"There! You've got it! Great job, Buddy!" James' and my excitement for telling our developmentally drunken four-year-old was mounting with each little paper square he found.

Then finally, "I found the last one!" Roo jumped up and down in delight at his completed task. He placed the final square on the poster board that now read:

U R GOING 2 BE A BIG BROTHER!

As we attempted desperately to have him read it aloud for the video and he kept missing the dramatic point we were trying to make. "I'm going to HAVE a big brother?! YES!"

"No, baby. That's not what it says ... it says you are going to BE a big brother!"

"To who?" His face smushed together as he tried to process the information. "We are having a baby." James pointed to me and then smiled his warmest, back and forth and back again, from me and Roo.

"Where?"

"In Mommy's tummy."

"No. Where is it going to live?"

"In our house! The baby will be a part of our family." I proclaimed, feeling a rush of excitement and simultaneous fear tingle through my body. Being pregnant and paralyzed is no joke.

Here we go again.

The whole scavenger hunt, aka. Pregnancy Reveal, took far longer than it should have. I snapped a very long video of the entire thing on my phone, strategic and hopeful that I could double as a videographer for the moment.

Later that evening, I sat down and cropped, sped up, and created a brief compilation of the night's events to share with my family and James'. The video was priceless. I hit SEND, and it all became real. The second your secret is not a secret anymore truly changes it and makes it much more: an experience. It felt like a sturdy vine growing up into the clouds, awaiting a smallish peddler to climb in search of his riches. An enormous vine that only exists in fairytales and imaginations. That was the sort of secret we were dealing with here. A secret that was right in front of all of us and terribly hard to keep anymore.

Within minutes, James' parents had video phoned us to congratulate the three of us on the news. Margot called, jumping up and down as well. My sister Abby said she totally knew it based on the old dress I wore a few months back, although truth be told I wasn't even pregnant at that point. My dad and Jackie clapped and wanted more details—or at least my dad did. He needed logistics, like always, and I felt prepared. Faye, now living in Germany with a family of her own, teared up and wished she were there. Everyone was just as elated as we were, and I was so relieved. That was, until I realized I hadn't heard from my mom.

Since my parents' divorce, she had done a fairly good job living alone. That is something I never thought she'd be able to manage. She bought her own condo, directly behind the house we grew up in and furnished it mostly with the artifacts from my childhood. She was now clean, sober, and still reaching for her way back into all of our lives.

It had been so long and so hard for so many years. And no matter how hard I tried to let go, I would never fully be able to relinquish all the scars and defects that were sewn directly to my heart itself. I wish so hard I could.

But I knew she was trying.

I knew she had nothing but love for my tiny family and me. I tried, like a clumsy trapeze artist, to hold on to the rope of hope and goodwill that was entertained by my mom.

It had been nearly twenty years since my mom hit her weakest and lowest point. Even covered with new memories and family photos, that pain will never truly fade away entirely.

Believe me, I tried. I tried for my sake, but mostly I tried for that sweet ol' Roo and his crazy Nana.

I tried.

Everything became just a bit harder, but more transparent, when my mom was diagnosed with diabetes nearly six years prior. We were at a family celebration at my house long before I met James, long before I could even dream of being a mom, and so many foreign moons ago. Like Jupiter's moons ago.

My mom arrived that Sunday afternoon with my aunt and uncles, grandparents, and cousins already present and in full celebration mode when the music literally stopped. My mom stood in the doorway with her skin drooping noticeably over her already-thin elbows. Her face, gaunt and green. She looked tired and weak, yet played a smile that couldn't really hold the tune as she tried.

But, oh how she tried.

I asked if she was alright, and she shooed me away to join in on the fun. Abby and I knew something just *wasn't* right. My uncle Charlie knew it too. He quickly thought of his own diagnoses of diabetes, and asked to check my mom's blood sugar. Lo and behold, her number was off the charts.

By the time I had her in front of a doctor at a nearby urgent care facility, it was revealed that her tested number would have put so many others in a coma. Her body had clearly been surviving with it for a while. Her body had tried so desperately not to waiver. For the first time I could remember ever, I recognized that my mom was strong.

Being diagnosed with diabetes was so hard for her at first. Understanding that carbohydrates and sugars are found in foods everywhere. Knowing that sometimes you need more and sometimes you need less. The education of it all had a mountainous learning curve, especially for my mom. From her years of self-torture, she had unintentionally lessened her abilities to understand through the constant poisoning of brain cells.

But she tried.

However, at this moment, as we sat answering phone calls and texts of love and joy, video calls and emails of elation and praise, my mom simply didn't reach out.

Something was wrong.

"Abby, have you heard from Mom?" I interrupted her as she continued on about all of the signs she simply *knew* that I was pregnant, and all the obvious wisdoms she had about her own two previous pregnancies.

"Wait, no. No, I haven't. I'll try to get a hold of her now."

"I already have. She didn't answer."

"Should I go over there?"

"Maybe? I'm sorry. You went over last time too." "I know. It's okay. I'll call you when I get there."

"Okay, thank you and sorry." We hung up the phone in an all too familiar fashion. A lulling panic blanketed over my excitement. The panic was fleeting, yet so sad. That panic did a U-turn, parked, and changed drivers altogether. The new driver was poised, unaffected, and incredibly stoic. Rather unfortunately, we had been down this road one too many times before.

Abby and I shared a tone of speech that was only turned on in moments like these. Abby had a low and slow tone blended to her otherwise normal higher-than-mine voice. Me, I would refer to my vocal substitution coming from my alter ego, "Robot Ry." My syllables were prominently paused, yet spoken with subtle energy. Once I started to recognize this certain voice of mine, I also realized that I couldn't possibly look anyone in the eyes during its activation. It was a fight-or-flight response that my body yearned for, but my brain just couldn't handle it. Autopilot initiated. Beep-boop-beep.

Hidden beneath my robot exterior, I recognized—quite possibly for the first time—that Abby was grown. She was a real, live get-yourself-out-of-bed-everyday-on-your-own-to-go-to-work-your-nine-to-five-workday certified grown-up. I'm not sure when it happened nor when I missed it, but she and I were now peers. Abby had come down, perhaps, an even windier and bumpier road than I had. She was the baby of the family that never got the instructions she needed to rise above for herself, yet there she was driving to take care of our ailing mom.

My mom tried to manage her diabetes in the best way she could, but that often ended up with an ambulance call and paramedic intervention. She too often found her way to a diabetic low, stumbling over words and chairs, and reminding me of an all too familiar tortured past. It seemed like such an unfortunate and unintentional torture for both Abby and me.

My mom did her best and overcame so much from those days. But it felt more like a masquerade ball with extravagant, glittery masks hiding the most gruesome creatures underneath. There was always a part of me that wondered if her body liked the feeling of that low blood sugar, giving her an accidental drunken state. I tried not to think like that.

There I was, so excited to expand our family, now so worried and wondering about my mom's uncooperative pancreas. I shushed the cerebral voices that told me that it wasn't fair. I hid back some old leftover tears from years come and gone, and went on with typing replies of our news.

I tried so hard to smile.

It wasn't ever easy. The moments when you aren't quite sure what is going on, when your mind wanders to deep and dark things you never want to mention. No matter how you try to hush them with distractions, they ooze through your brain folds and make everything achy and horrid. *Stop it! She's fine. She always is ... so lucky. What if she's not lucky this time? Don't think like that.*

I was trying. Trying hard not to lessen my smile from the news for Roo. Trying so hard not to think the worst. The subtle, yet powerful act of *trying* has always fueled me. It was the reason I rose above my accident; it was the reason I chose to compete in swimming again. It was also ultimately responsible for the family that James and I were growing.

Emotion has a way of sneaking back into the conversation, when Abby called to say that our mom was okay. The emotions were a full spectrum of things from relief to anger, from thankful to fear.

Sure enough, her blood sugar was low, and she was unresponsive to the world around her. Unresponsive. The world may as well have froze in time for her while grape juice and fruit chews worked their sugary magic to bring my mom back to it all, and to us. Yes, she was *okay*. But that was part of the problem.

I thanked Abby again, in my Robot Ry-business-as-usual type manner, and made plans for her and my nieces to visit over the weekend. James rubbed my back and apologized to me. But was it for what happened with my mom? Was it for diabetes itself? Or was it for being forced back to my scared teenage self that he would never truly know nor understand?

Any way, I apologized back. His soft, whiskery smile brought my attention back to Roo, who was now playing quietly with some die-cast cars on the living room rug.

My problem with my mom being *okay* wasn't a cruel attempt at me getting back at her all these years. It was less emotional than that. When my mom would suffer from her diabetic attacks, she would be the only one who actually would do no outward suffering. She didn't remember them. Or her blank stares or wobbling stance. Didn't remember her slurred, cross words. And she definitely didn't remember making us all so upset. All of this made it easy for her to blow it off and return to her own vicious cycle of diabetes-style Russian roulette. She did not remember those diabetic lows, just like she didn't remember when she drank. She did not remember things.

I would never not remember.

Later that evening, my mom would call me, overly overjoyed and overreactive for our news. So typical. She was that way with just about everything. It could be the weather that caused her to hoot and cheer, or just some googly-eyed craft that Roo and I pasted together. Really, it didn't take much. And unfortunately for everyone, that excited tone could unintentionally trigger me right back to being "Robot Ry" once again. I have never received praise well, not from my mom and not from anyone else. It doesn't suit me. I have no space for it.

Nevertheless, this instance gave way to so much verbal praise. She would howl and holler, and she would be the best cheerleader for our news. She would not, however, make a single mention of the scare that she gave us earlier that night. I'm not sure which of it all was most upsetting.

I wanted so deeply to feel that joy the way that she did, but I just couldn't. She could speak to her misgivings, and would much rather move along. I guess, in some ways, that's exactly how I function too. It's survival. Growing up, our family was made that way. I didn't mention it either, and the whole emotion of it all sat in the form of the welling tears in my eyes as I spoke. Those tears didn't dare come out. I wouldn't let them. I chose rather to focus on the cheerleader at the other end and thanked her for her excitement.

I live emotionally and love purely. But I also lean toward the upbringing of my stoic father and don't-worry-about-a-thing mother. It is so amazing how, no matter what you do to keep your parental demons out of your own persona, they still might be there anyway. I know better than to be like that. Yet it's like trying to tell yourself to take the other foot before the one. You just can't walk like that.

When it all comes down to it, every part of both my father and my mother has made me *me*. Not only in a genetic, blue-eyed recessive sense, but also in the impact of upbringing. I appreciate it all. All of the good and the bad, sprinkled in with the DNA has created my life—my decisions, my consequences, as well as all the acceptances in between. They are unexplainable connections. They will always be my family.

But it is with my full understanding of family, the one I had helped create for myself, and where I truly live. It is everything. To create life and connect with it so deeply that the line is quite blurry of where you stop and they begin. That is the family that I have made.

There I sat in front of my laptop computer with exclamation point replies of our newest addition on the way. I watched my four-year-old play gently on our clearance center Persian-version rug, and catching James' glances at my belly. I knew that I truly had everything I had ever wanted.

I would have to continue on with both the struggles of my past and present families, but without both, my life simply just wouldn't be. I may never fully understand why things happen for each of us, and if I truly just had *bad luck* that night our car rolled through the air. But the world that now existed, around me and *for* me, made all of that not matter so much anymore. That past was not my present, but at the same time, it absolutely was. Everything about my past generated my present. And, I wouldn't change any of it, for fear that it would affect that ultimate outcome of my present world.

I closed my eyes and listened hard for that life growing inside of my belly. Fighting yet another tear forming from deep inside, I took one big breath in and smiled for my new baby, and for our budding family. At the present, that was *my* present and all that mattered.

"Here we go, little one," I whispered softly, as so James nor Roo would hear. This whisper was meant for someone else. A whisper meant for that slight little baby, no larger than a lime, hiding inside of me. "I am your mom."

Sitting alone in the soon-to-be baby room moonlighting as an office, I clicked the desk light off to leave, yet lingered. I circled my pointer finger as if I were writing a letter on the desk next to my computer. In brief, illegible and invisible cursive, I spelled out: *Always try.*

a birth of things

GROWING ANOTHER HUMAN INSIDE OF YOU is actually a lot like writing a book. Retelling my story is something that sat inside of me for so long. It grew slowly and took shape from every piece of life. It was painful. There was so much deleted and hidden away. It was so agonizing, but in the end, that pain was good. The pain needed a house, somewhere to lay its weary head at night. A book. Something that I had been carrying with me for so long.

SOMETHING THAT I HAD BEEN CARRYING with me for so long. The weight of my body felt like it had doubled. It was heavy–I was heavy. My growing baby inside of me was pushing on every part of me, yet it was remarkably bearable knowing the innocent source.

"You scared me." I sounded so out of breath. I always sounded out of breath those days. I blamed the tiny body inside of me. It was using all my organs to snuggle with, including my anciently scarred lungs. James had walked in the room holding an outdated rocking chair. He startled me in my thoughts, and I smiled at him for bringing me out of my daydream.

The room was painted a faint, yet vibrant orange with the hope of stimulating brains for productivity, as it was meant to be a workable office space. I found so much energy in that room, both for working and mind-wandering alike. It was where I hid away from the rest of the world for thirty seconds of self-reflection, list-making, or baby-dreaming.

"I'm sorry, babe. I didn't mean to. I was just bringing in that old rocking chair that you asked me about." He motioned to the rocking chair that he had now placed in the corner of the room. It rocked subtly from the motion of it being stationed on the floor, as though it was nodding to me in agreeance of all things.

"Thank you. It'll be perfect in here. I can't believe we still have it." I began patting and releasing dust from the seat and back cushions. The rocking chair was missing both of its padded arms and covered in the dust of years of garage life. It had been stuck between some worn boxes labeled, "School Work Stuff" and "Stupid Kitchen Décor" and smelled strongly of James' old Dodge truck that, too, made its permanent home in our garage.

"Yeah, it's pretty dusty. But it's still in good shape. You should sit. You look like you could use a rest." James was right, but with my hormones, I couldn't help but be slightly annoyed.

Forever holding a sitting position in my chair, left me even less available space in my abdominal cavity in my current basketball-belly-state. I was so uncomfortable and so swollen. It was painful. Everything hurt.

My belly cut off circulation to my already blood-starved legs. My bladder was squeezed to death at every given second of every day. I was perpetually begging the question, "Is that pee or did my water break?" So much so that I had purchased drugstore pH indicator strips to attempt to decipher the fluid, nearly every single day. I had developed heart palpitations, which terrified me enough to visit a specialist about it. I sat hooked up to a contraction monitor every three days, wishing the entire time that the lines on the paper would dance out of control. They didn't.

I ached all over on the outside, yet I was trying to maintain the coziest of environments for my growing baby on the inside. I pictured a white fleece blanket with little red hearts, wrapping him up and rocking him to sleep. I read him books and sang him songs. I read him poetry. It all made me realize, I owed it to him, and to Roo to finish that something I had started long before I even suspected them as characters myself. Characters that changed my world.

CHARACTERS THAT CHANGED MY WORLD. I was always dazzled by concocted *characters* and loved how writing could give life to my own imagination and inspiration.

When I was twelve years old, I kept a pocket-sized, pastel pink notebook on my shelf. It wasn't hidden like my diary, but it also wasn't advertised to anyone either. It sat cozy between my Snow White and Pollyanna Madame Alexander dolls, as I'm sure somewhere they felt like the heroines I needed to protect such a treasure.

The treasure? Words.

I began creating short quotes that I felt would motivate and inspire silly little prepubescents like myself. Those short quotes metamorphosed into poetry and verse, as I metamorphosed as well.

Back then, I didn't see the power that those short writings had given me. I was young and didn't grasp the sheer command that creating strands of words could have. I was writing to get rid of pain. I wrote in that pastel notebook in the same manner in which I brushed my teeth. It was habitual, it was routine. I never thought any more of it. That's where it all began.

Until one day, that notebook into my soul was gone. I had been released from the hospital after my accident, shuffled into my grandiose basement apartment, and I never saw the notebook nor my words ever again. My words were lost.

MY WORDS WERE LOST. I was caught in searching for those words that are so deep and emotive, that there aren't actually any words ever assigned.

The rocking chair was something that Roo had been rocked in for hours and hours when he was young. That rocking chair gave me another chair in my life with a specific purpose. I would transfer out of my wheelchair, exchange it for the rocker as I was exchanging my entire life for my life as a mom. That single-duty, deliberate rocker gave me new purpose, and I took that job of sway so seriously. But once he outgrew his crib, he had outgrown wanting to rock as well.

Those milestones have always been so bittersweet. Watching your baby learn and grow, and outgrow. Watching him take possibly his last bottle, or that last nap in his crib. When I closed my eyes, I could almost remember that last rocking chair moment with Roo. Almost. I have forced myself to be good at grabbing those moments as they happened. Life can be so fleeting otherwise.

In recognizing those firsts and lasts with Roo, I vowed to hold on to baby moments much better with NuNu. I was to be keen to the potency of *the lasts* with him. Those moments became stories. They were all captured by me and for me. Those stories *were* me.

THOSE STORIES *WERE* ME. Secretly, I have always wanted to be a writer, even when it felt like the universe didn't agree. I had this English teacher once in high school that absolutely despised how I spun words together. Perhaps we also didn't see eye-to-eye because I came to her class just after lunch and the down-spiral from morning swim practice. My digesting stomach and the beaming afternoon sunlight made it all too easy to doze off in her class. Nonetheless, I took great pride in my work. But from the moment I turned in my masterpiece, it would be returned as garbage. Each written assignment was markedly torn apart by her, every single one. There wasn't a sole paper that year that she didn't make me rewrite.

It made me angry, and it made me want to not care. But I did care. And, damnit, I wanted her approval. I would receive my assignment back every single time, with a note at the top of the page: "I stopped reading here. Revise for tomorrow." There was never more of an explanation in that red curly writing of hers. And I was far too embarrassed and emotionally stunted to contemplate asking further. I just did as told. My parents complained that I was wasting computer paper.

I went that entire year afraid and indignant of my writing. When she lectured in class, I chose to hear her voice with a harsh Russian accent—verbal daggers about serial commas and progressive tenses. That made me feel better for some reason, but I realized that I never wanted to feel that way about my writing again. I needed to find a way to feel okay.

I NEEDED TO FIND A WAY TO FEEL OKAY. I dusted off the pad-less, wooden arms of the rocker and pushed it into motion ever so gently. It wooed back and forth so delicately and subtly. It lulled only air, but gave me such a calm notion that I couldn't help but climb in.

Having a baby is not a task for a weak person. Nor is raising a baby. I hold that title with much pride. And with so much fear. Unbeknownst to him, Roo experienced his first four years of life with my silent assurance that he would surely die any moment. I barely slept or breathed fully those first few years. My imagination was monstrous then. Having him made me realize how afraid of life I truly was.

I pushed my fingers against my thigh to get the chair to start rocking. I envisioned my legs pumping against the motion to carry it for hours, but I knew my fingers were going to have to push it again soon. The rocking was so soothing. And with my legs propped up on my chair, I felt so calm and open. But even in the calmest of moments, there is always a chance for that fear to settle back in.

Once you have something you love, you inevitably risk losing it.

Having been suffocated so abruptly as a sixteen-year-old with that realization, it wasn't something that I could let go of. I was forced to learn how to live through that fear.

I was about to have another baby and another life that would certainly suffer if it weren't for all of my worrying. I had to trust the universe that my world was going to be okay. That this baby was going to be okay. I patted my stomach and closed my eyes. The rocking chair made me rest. Swaying back and forth, those worries lulled because I realized that they had no business there in the first place. The fear, although a good sifter of emotions and priorities, was only going to keep me from being alright. And, right now, I needed to feel more than okay. I needed to feel *good*.

I NEEDED TO FEEL GOOD, so I needed to *do* something. An idea came to me while I was still on bed rest in my solo-single family home in the mountains. "Project ME" was a name that I coined when planning my return to normalcy, a journey that was to be chronicled in a blog that I kept. It was meant to take some of the fear I had grown in the last months of bed rest and squash it hard.

It was after nearly nine months of wound healing, realizing that my mind still had some healing to do of its own. I took action. I began to write again.

Roosting on the theme of trying something new every day for thirty days, I figured that would be a really good way to jump back into life. Seeing as I had just wasted away the last three-quarters of a year, I wasn't about to delay anything for another second.

Jumping both at the chance to finally *do* something as well as write about it, I rose out of my depression rather quickly.

I celebrated a Day of Silence. I became a vegan for a day. I watched a foreign film with the subtitles covered so I couldn't read them nor understand what was spoken. I wrote a letter to the driver of my accident to let her know that I never blamed her. I left sticky notes of encouragement in the grocery aisles of my local store, for anyone willing to stop and take a look. I visited my grandma's grave.

There were thirty days of well-thought-out explorations. Thirty days of reflections, written out as thirty blogs, doubling as my world-wide diary. It was much simpler than that too—it was thirty days of *living*. The whole thing was as cathartic as it was capturing. Blogging was the way to capture my writing. Feasibly forever.

FEASIBLY FOREVER. It was how I thought of this pregnancy as I had extremely real fears about the outcome. If I didn't know I was in labor before, what was going to stop this baby from just sneaking right out of me in my sleep? I had learned with Roo that there was so much luck involved. I couldn't possibly believe that I would be so lucky twice.

Thankfully, Dr. Berg had conceded my pleas and scheduled an induction the first day of my 39th week. With the knowledge that Roo was born at 38 weeks, it was only a sheer gauze shawl of comfort.

Ironically, all the planning distracted me from a sharp nudgy pain that came and went through the day prior to the induction. That baby never seemed to sit square within me. He always seemed to find a snuggle spot on one side or the other. It was easy to blame him and his positional restlessness.

That nudgy pain though. It felt hard and fast, and I could feel it inside my teeth. It was a feeling that I hadn't ever felt. But it didn't hurt, so it was easy for me to ignore.

I went about my day.

After coaching a full swim meet, wheeling up and down the humid pool deck, James and I settled in for dinner on an outside patio at our favorite eatery. We had already dropped off Roo at my dad's house as planned and chose to enjoy a last minute alone, just the two of us. We clanked glasses. We joked about the arugula in between James' front teeth and it foreseeably being our last date for several years. *Cheers!*

Little did we know, NuNu was starting his final descent. He felt no need to wait for any scheduled induction. He knew how to make a jump on his desperately over-planned mom.

That night, I woke up panicking about having a baby in my sleep for the very last time. My sleep had been disjointed and worrisome for months. I had learned with Roo that I truly didn't know what a contraction felt like and that scared me beyond any demanded sleep.

As I felt down underneath the covers for any signs of life or wetness, I knew we would have a baby the very next day. No more worrying and wondering. No more speculating or false planning. It was so relieving after nine-plus months of perpetual panic. I fell back into the best sleep I had experienced in years. I was about to meet my baby, to give life to the very thing my body was working so hard to comfort and grow.

I WAS ABOUT TO FINISH MY BOOK, to give life to the very thing my mind was working so hard to comfort and grow. Giving life to strings of words, creating glorious images for others to interpret has always empowered me. And, what's even more empowering—is when those words are stories from your own reality and memories. Storytelling.

The first known form dates back before we can even be sure. Storytelling has been an art long before there were notions of literature and fine arts. Being passed down through generations, reaching all nooks of the world, blanketing its own magical fairy dust on any ear that chooses to listen.

There were sticky note stories, stuck to Roo's dry erase board in his room with chapter titles scrawled in all sorts of pens of the day. There were stories that I used for classroom speeches about car safety. There were also stories I didn't dare tell a soul. But it was time. I had to do it.

Taking that art of storytelling I made it my own. For something so universal and ancient, I simply couldn't deny my own choice of art. To honor the legacy of the story. To translate my own timeless tale from my own memory. To create something that has roots in the earliest of man. I chose this moment to write—and write, and write, and write. Something started to make sense.

SOMETHING STARTED TO MAKE SENSE. The achy pains were more and more frequent. They radiated and resonated all the way inside of my teeth. They weren't subsiding, in fact, they were amplifying. By the time I made it to the hospital in the morning, I was in active, but silent, labor. It had been knocking on my door, waiting for me to answer. *How could I have ignored it?* I was so hyper-focused on acknowledging when I was in labor, that I inadvertently threw up a "No Solicitors" sign and peered only through the peephole in the door.

My body and brain connection had fooled me once again. Nearly an entire life of doing so, this time, however, I got it backwards. This time, my body was telling me everything I needed, and I chose not to sense it at all.

I casually told the nurse about my newish side pains after being checked into my room. I didn't realize that they were happening more frequently, but they were. And I didn't realize, those aches had a name and a warning for me.

With a questioning "hmm," she checked well underneath the sheets only to be shocked into sympathetic response from both of us. She had to tell me what I was feeling. It was time to go.

"He's coming!" the nurse's voice shook. She was struggling to keep from sounding panicked herself. "Now?!" I questioned as I already knew it to be true.

Without even getting to enjoy the soft sheets and framed flowers on the walls, I was rushed into a smaller examination room to get prepped for delivery. Suddenly, everyone was alarmed at the progress my non-induction had gained.

I had driven myself, figuring that the induction could take a while, so luckily, James had arrived just in time. He joined the delivery staff in the tiny exam room that really should only hold about three people—not ten.

Before I knew it, James was holding my hand and encouraging me to push. The doctors and nurses were surrounding me to do the same. With Roo, I, at least, had enough physical function to push *enough*. I didn't quite understand it, but my brain spoke softly, just enough to my body to tell it what to do. Knowing that made me proud. It made me prouder than if I had just gotten up and walked out of the building myself.

I bared down once more. My teeth clenched as sweat dripped from my forehead down my temple. I held my breath until I couldn't anymore. A sigh came straight from my diaphragm, floating its way out of my mouth at the same time my sweet baby sighed his first desire of life.

The world was unexpectedly quiet. Shushed to allow for this new life to connect to it. I held him and kissed him softly on his nose. James cradled his tiny head and welcomed him to the world. My dad and Jackie greeted him with soft smiles and his new big brother, Roo. My mom and Abby smiled just the same, as there was no need for anything else at that moment.

To this day, NuNu is forever swift, sneaky, and full of all the love. It was all so fast, that it was hard for me to even grab a memory of it all. But that is exactly how this baby chose to come into the world with us. Our family was complete.

THE BOOK WAS COMPLETE. I wrote and wrote and wrote, until it finally felt like I had put everything into words that needed them. It was on paper, hundreds of thousands of words, ready for the world. Writing it down, my stories gave me the capacity to reflect and learn. I was able, for the first time, to make sense of my choices, my adventures, my relationships. *My life.* What I learned was that I had a lot of strength resting in the most uneasy of places. Those stories. I created so many victories for myself in instances where others might see them as something entirely different: struggles.

Creating something, whether it be a human being or a compilation of stories—or something entirely different altogether is what life is about. For as long as people have been dancing on this earth, they have been creating. That is what keeps us going, makes us whole, and separates us from the rest of the animal kingdom. That simple ability to have the means to create is the most powerful potential energy in the entire universe, but it comes at a cost. Watch out folks, because it causes you to *feel*.

True vulnerability is a wake-up call that you don't provoke. It causes you to react. Makes you feel and do something. Challenges your everything. It breaks you and creates you all in the same breath. And what you do with that—that is strength. And that is living.

I wanted to be a mom when I grew up.

I wanted to be a writer when I grew up.

There was a deep fear within me that I could never be either one.

Notwithstanding, I am not a chair anymore.

And even though the writing has stopped, my story certainly isn't over.

GRATITUDE

JUST AS ALL MEMOIRS GO, this book wouldn't have been written if it weren't for every single life that has ever touched mine. I mean that wholly. Regardless if I made you an actual character and gave you a fake name, or not–you were no more or less important to this work. And, likewise you were important to me. I wish I could hug each of you for being something to me. And, it doesn't matter how long or in what manner we were connected–the important thing is that we CONNECTED. That is all life is really about anyways, isn't it?

But there are a few extra hugs I will dole out.

To my 3 little bears–Andrew, Van, and Orren. You three changed my story and my life in ways that I could have never believed for myself. You made my story heroic. You made my story a love story. And, you made my story complete.

To my Grandmas. Yes, plural. Even though I only spoke of one grandma in my book, I really molded both of my grandmothers into this character, as they were both so necessary to give credit to in my upbringing.

To my family—my dad, my sister, and my mom. Sharing this book with the world was difficult for me because I knew that it would bring up difficult conversations for us all. I so hope that my words can bring us closer together as we all navigate this modern, discombobulated family of today. I am who I am today because of each of you.

Mom, some of my words may be relentless to read. Some of my words may feel sharp and twisting. But please know that those feelings truly matter to me, and that this wasn't done without a lot of lost sleep and stomach aches. I truly hope that those who read my words recognize how hard you've tried and what a loving Nana you are to the world.

To my longest forever friendships—Erin and Sarah. Whenever I have felt in my life that I had nothing to stand on, nothing to hold me up, you were there. Together, we have been silly and stupid, we have been magical and whimsical. Erin, you are the only person I can count on to be eternally honest with me. Sarah, you know my words before I know them myself. I am a lucky girl to have known you both for most of my life.

To my miracle manuscript workers—Polly Letofsky, Jennifer Bisbing, Cathy Spader, Erin Fletcher, and Julia Seldin. I am absolutely positive this book would have never been finished without you. And, I am sure you are all nodding your heads right now. It has been well over a decade of rewriting and manipulation. You all had an amazing presence in my work at the most remarkable of times.

And, finally to the champion cheerleaders who have always been there for me. You have been rooting me on and clapping my way towards various endeavors and adventures that wouldn't have happened without your encouragement. I can hear great applause right now from the Foxridge Swim Club, from Cherry Creek High School prior students and staff, from my Swim Dogs Swim Team family, and from pivotal (yet individual) connections that have carried me through and cheered me to the absolute best of my world.

This work is my heart and my soul. It is all because of *you*.

ABOUT THE AUTHOR

HER CALL TO WRITE A BOOK was a quiet, yet constant voice that Ryan Rae Harbuck finally listened to. And after writing as much as she could between coaching swim practices and conducting toddler craft times, *when i grow up i want TO BE A CHAIR* was born.

A Colorado native, Ryan has always found solace in the mountain air and has always been up for an outdoor challenge—as far as her wheelchair wheels could take her, or beyond. She has been a teacher and a swim coach, but enjoys being Mom the most. She and her husband, Andrew live in Denver with their two mudslinging, car-vrooming young boys.

Ryan is available to share her stories in publications and book readings. To learn more, please visit her website at www.ryanraeharbuck.com.

9 780578 983738